JACK LONDON'S
CALIFORNIA

George Wharton James, an Englishman-turned-California-writer, with Jack London
in September 1911, on the London ranch in the Valley of the Moon, Sonoma County
California.

JACK LONDON'S CALIFORNIA

The Golden Poppy and Other Writings

EDITED WITH AN INTRODUCTION BY

SAL NOTO

◆

BEAUFORT BOOKS
Publishers · New York

All photographs (except pp. 70 and 140) courtesy of the Estate of Irving
Shepard

Library of Congress Cataloging-in-Publication Data

London, Jack, 1876–1916.
   Jack London's California.

   1. California—Literary collections.   I. Noto, Sal.
II. Title.
PS3523.046A6   1986   818'.5209   85-26720
ISBN 0-8253-0356-7

Published in the United States by Beaufort Books Publishers, New York.

Designed by Jill Weber

Printed in the U.S.A.   First Edition

10 9 8 7 6 5 4 3 2 1

Once again, to Nancy, Andrew, and my mother and father.

Contents

Acknowledgments

This collection would not have been possible without the help and encouragement of Milo Shepard, Executor of the Trust of Irving Shepard. In Jack London tradition, Milo always left "the latch string out on the gate" whenever I called upon him at the London Ranch in California's Valley of the Moon.

My appreciation is also extended to Russ Kingman, proprietor of the Jack London Bookstore in Glen Ellen, California, who responded expeditiously to my urgent requests for photographs (in his care by the Shepard Trust) and several of the illustrations that appear in this collection. For the early photograph of Jack London in the Sierras, I am grateful to Arnold and Virginia Applegarth of San Jose, California.

Earle Labor and Howard Lachtman always gave freely and generously of their time and critical expertise by making valuable suggestions while the work was in progress. Sara Hodson of the Huntington Library in San Marino, California, was most gracious and helpful when called upon to trace the most elusive information about London.

Others who have helped immeasurably over the years (either by example or in the subtle ways that make a work of this type possible) are Carl Bernatovech, Jackie Koenig, Joseph Izzo, Jr., James Sisson, Dick Weiderman, Stanley Wertheim, Mark Zamen, and "The Crowd" at the Quality Café.

Also, I'd like to thank my good friend Irv Koppel, with whom this whole grand adventure with Jack London began one summer afternoon in San Francisco back in 1962.

Finally, my greatest debt is to my wife, Nancy, who was always encouraging and optimistic and helped in a host of ways throughout the entire experience.

Introduction

"Behold! I have moved!" Jack London exclaimed in a letter written to his good friend and literary confidant, Cloudesley Johns, in February 1902. "Am beautifully located in new house," he continued in excited brevity. "We have a big living room, every inch of it, floor and ceiling finished in redwood . . . The rest of the house is finished in redwood too, and very, very comfortable. We have . . . a big clump of magnificent pines, flowers, and flowers galore . . . half of ground in bearing orchard and half sprinkled with California poppies; we are twenty-four minutes from the door to the heart of Oakland and an hour and five minutes to San Francisco . . . our view commands all of San Francisco for a sweep of thirty or forty miles, and all the opposing shores such as Marin County and Mount Tamalpais. . . ."

If London sounded exuberant, he had every good reason; he was just beginning to experience success as a writer. He had recently celebrated his twenty-sixth birthday, and could already boast of a remarkable number of short stories and articles, plus two books to his credit. In addition, he was the proud father of a one-year-old daughter, and for the first time in his life, he was enjoying the luxury of a comfortable home in a setting which exceeded his fondest dreams.

This newfound home in Piedmont Heights, "The Bungalow," as it was called, became a Sunday afternoon and Wednesday evening rendezvous for London's growing circle of friends—writers, artists, intellectuals—"The Crowd," as they were known. They included George Sterling, the Byronesque poet and protégé of Ambrose Bierce; James Hopper, another aspiring author and later a journalist and short story writer; Xavier Martinez, the flamboyant Mexican-Indian artist; lovely Blanche Partington, sometime poet and critic; and a host of others.

"The Crowd" often gathered at the Londons' home to tramp through the poppy-laden fields on picnics, fly kites from the hillsides, and visit Joaquin Miller, the aging "poet of the Sierras" at his nearby retreat. It was a happy and prosperous time for London. He was writing feverishly, and reveled in the countrylike atmosphere where he could breathe the fresh California air and have a splendid view of San Francisco Bay at the same time.

London was always proud to say that he was first and foremost a Californian, and with rich material at hand, he drew heavily from personal experiences in his native state for much of what he wrote. So it is not surprising that over half of his books contain something concerning the people, events, and landscape of the Golden State during that colorful and sometimes turbulent period at the turn of the century. This collection brings together the best of his California writing.

Along with the title piece, "The Golden Poppy," included are excerpts from *The Valley of the Moon* and *Martin Eden*, two novels with strong, class-conscious themes written against a vivid California background. Nowhere else is London's own story of succeeding in the "writing game" better told than in *Martin Eden*, his thinly disguised autobiography. This work remains the favorite of many London aficionados, but not because it is a flawless novel. Structural problems aside, the story has universal appeal because of its compelling force, and a "rags to riches" theme drawn from the author's own experience.

Selections from the novel *Burning Daylight* have been included because at least half of the action takes place in the San Francisco Bay Area with some beautiful and lyrical descriptions of the Valley of the Moon, the author's home for the last eleven years of his life.

London wrote nearly 200 short stories represented here by the fine descriptive tale "All Gold Canyon," followed by two stories from *Tales of the Fish Patrol*, "A Raid on the Oyster Pirates" and "Demetrios Contos."

Among the shorter selections, "Small-Boat Sailing" could not be omitted; the humorous, relaxed, and informative travelogue "Navigating Four Horses North of the Bay" captures London and his entourage on a three-month trip through California's magnificent redwood country; and his exuberant review of a California classic (Frank Norris's *The Octopus*) stands as a classic in its own right. Finally, "The Story of an Eyewitness," a special magazine article on the San Francisco earthquake, is included. This is Jack London's dramatic account of the aftermath of the powerful 1906 earthquake and subsequent fire which left the city in ruins. Roaming the streets amid the rubble and charred ruins was no easy task for the sensitive au-thor-journalist. After all, the city was his birthplace.

Jack London grew up in California when the state was just begin-ning to shake free of the rowdy image created by the surge of gold-seekers and settlers that began in 1848. The western frontier, now spanned by the railroads, was disappearing. Likewise, California was settling down. Newcomers could take stock of the unspoiled land-scape and potential greatness of the "Golden Land by the Sundown Shore." Even an aging Ralph Waldo Emerson saw the face of things to come. In 1871, during his only visit to the state, he prophesied, "There is an awe and terror lying over this new garden, all empty as yet of any adequate people, yet with the assured future in Amer-ican hands; unequaled in climate and production . . . I should think no young man would come back from it."

The nascent state of California that Emerson saw had barely 600,000 people within its boundaries. Thirty years later, when Lon-don was just beginning to make a name for himself in the literary world, the population had almost tripled. A new breed of people from across the continent and from abroad wanted their fair share of this remarkable land, basking lazily in the sun by the Pacific. Among the new arrivals, there were many who were hardworking and ambitious, and a few of the unscrupulous. Opportunities, as Emerson had foreseen, appeared unlimited for everyone. But this new home for a host of restless, transplanted people was not with-out its share of "growing pains." And this was the California that London knew first-hand and wrote about.

Born in San Francisco on January 12, 1876, John Griffith London was the illegitimate son of Flora Wellman, an émigré from Massil-lon, Ohio, and William H. Chaney, an itinerant astrologer. Chaney denied that he fathered the child, claiming that he was impotent while living with Flora. Shirking any responsibility, he fled shortly after the birth, and there is no evidence that Flora or son ever saw him again. Eight months later, Flora married John London, a wid-ower with several children, and "Johnny" (as he was called at the time) acquired his stepfather's surname.

The wanderlust that London later exhibited was probably influ-enced by his early years, which were rootless and unstable. His family frequently moved within the San Francisco Bay Area—in and around Oakland, Alameda, and San Mateo, trying one venture after another in pursuit of a decent living. In the Livermore Valley, he tended bees for a time during one of their farm ventures and whiled away the lonely hours reading and dreaming of far-off places. But the farm proved to be a failure, the family returned to Oakland, and the adolescent London worked at a variety of jobs, including setting pins in a bowling alley and selling newspapers on the streets to supplement the family income.

When he was fifteen, he became an oyster pirate on San Francisco Bay, searching for excitement and easy but unlawful profits. Later, he joined the California Fish Patrol, a group that attempted to enforce law and order upon the Greeks, Italians, and Chinese who plundered the inland waters for salmon, shrimp, and oysters. These early experiences of navigating the choppy waters from Alviso to Benicia fostered a lifelong love of sailing.

At the age of seventeen, he signed on as an able-bodied seaman on a sealing schooner for a seven-month cruise to Japan and the Bonin Islands in the North Pacific. When he returned, the only work available was heavy physical labor. Among other things, he shoveled coal in an electric power plant, was a longshoreman, and worked long hours for little pay in a jute mill. He would later refer to these hard times as his "work-beast days."

In 1894, during a nationwide economic depression, London joined the West Coast contingent of Coxey's Industrial Army, a mass of unemployed men who planned a protest march to Washington, D.C. But, at the time, the eighteen-year-old vagabond was more interested in high adventure than social problems, and he abandoned the group midway and tramped on his own to the East Coast. At Niagara Falls he was arrested for vagrancy and sentenced to a month in the Erie County Penitentiary in Pennsylvania. Upon his release, he rode the rails back home to Oakland. This "tramping" experience, especially the interlude in prison, made an indelible impression upon him. For one thing, it helped to convert London to socialism, which would become an important theme in some of his writing, and also convinced him that he had to further his education if he was ever going to amount to anything.

Though he was nineteen years old and certainly older than his peers in worldly experiences, he enrolled for a year in Oakland High School. Later, he entered a "cramming" academy, hoping to bypass two more years of secondary schooling for a diploma. But even the pace at the academy proved too slow. London wanted a shortcut to an education, and with great determination and self-discipline, he studied prodigiously for three months on his own, passed the University of California entrance exams, and enrolled at the Berkeley campus during the fall term of 1896. But financial problems at home plagued him, and the course work, which was uninspiring to the impatient London, became intolerable and he dropped out after a semester. Shortly thereafter, news of the gold discovery in the

Klondike reached California. Always ready to break away from the routine and mundane, he was soon grubstaked and bound for the Yukon.

Although London found little gold during his nearly yearlong stay in the Canadian wilderness, his time in the Northland proved to be one of the most important events of his life. "It was in the Klondike that I found myself," he said later. "There . . . you get your perspective. I got mine." It is doubtful that he would have achieved the success and worldwide recognition he later enjoyed as a writer had he never gone to the gold fields.

When London returned to Oakland in the summer of 1898, he was armed with fresh material from his Yukon and Alaskan experiences. By this time, he had also steeped himself in philosophic and scientific works on evolutionary thought of the day, particularly Herbert Spencer's *First Principles* and Charles Darwin's *The Origin of Species*. With renewed confidence he began to write with fervor, and gradually his stories began to appear in such magazines as the *Overland Monthly* and the prestigious *Atlantic Monthly*. When he was twenty-four, his first book, *The Son of the Wolf*, a collection of well-crafted Northland tales, was published by Houghton-Mifflin. The book received favorable reviews, and London was on his way as a professional writer.

At the same time, eager to become a father, he impulsively married Bessie Maddern, a staid, well-educated young woman. Always forthright, London made it clear that though he liked and respected her, and felt she would make a good wife and mother, he was not in love. The marriage produced two daughters (Joan, born in 1901, and Becky, in 1902), but it was doomed from the outset. Temperamentally, London and Bessie were poles apart. During this time, however, in a burst of creative energy, he wrote *The Call of the Wild*, the great short novel that brought him worldwide acclaim.

Shortly after his separation from Bessie in 1903, he admonished a friend, "It's all right for a man sometimes to marry philosophically, but remember, it's damned hard on the woman." London had learned his lesson the hard way; the next time he would marry for love.

In 1905, anxious to escape from the domestic problems and notoriety created by the failure of his first marriage (by this time his name made "good copy" for newspapers across the country), London moved from Oakland to a rural retreat in Sonoma County. A relationship with Charmian Kittredge, the new woman in his life, had evolved into something much deeper than a casual affair. During his visits with the spunky Miss Kittredge and her relatives (at the latter's Wake Robin Lodge in Glen Ellen in the Valley of the Moon), London found himself fascinated by the beauty and seclusion of this countryside's wooded hills, quiet streams, and scattered orchards and vineyards. This was a sharp departure from his youthful distaste for life in the country, but he was mellowing and saw the land from a much broader perspective.

By now, his career was well established, and London began thinking seriously about acquiring the first "real" home of his own (he had always been a tenant). He was making plans to "anchor good and solid, and . . . for keeps." Often living beyond his means, partly because he gave financial support to numerous members of his family, he wrote to his publisher requesting royalties he had earned. "For a long time I have been keeping . . . in mind the idea of settling down somewhere in the country. I am in a beautiful part of California now, and I have my eye on several properties, one of which I intend to buy. . . ."

The publisher complied, and London soon became the proud owner of 127 acres of wooded and open hill country in Glen Ellen. He was also trying desperately to "write his way out" of the Klondike—to break away from stories and themes which had made his name synonymous with the Northland saga. Before the year ended, he had also made a cross-country lecture tour, married Charmian on the day after his divorce from Bessie became final, and was ready to become a full-time resident of Glen Ellen. With his spirited new wife, who seemed to be the perfect "Mate" (as he called her), London began making big plans for the future.

In early 1906, one of his more grandiose ideas began to take form. He and Charmian planned a seven-year cruise around the world in what would be their two-masted ketch, called the Snark (from Lewis Carroll's mock-epic poem, The Hunting of the Snark). The purpose of the trip was twofold: to provide "big moments of living" in the far reaches of the world and to absorb rich material for London's writing wherever they went.

Unfortunately, the trip was troubled from the outset. There were constant delays in building the vessel: even the 1906 San Francisco earthquake caused a major setback in construction. Also, the final cost of more than $30,000 greatly exceeded the original estimate of $7,000, a considerable sum in those days. Creditors were nipping at his heels, and the local newspapers began to label the venture as "London's folly."

Nevertheless, the Snark finally sailed from the Port of Oakland and through the Golden Gate on April 23, 1907. Major repairs then had to be made in Hawaii, but ship and crew ultimately reached the Marquesas, Tahiti, Samoa, the Fijis, New Hebrides, and the Solomon Islands. After two years, they reached Australia, but were heartbroken when the trip had to be abandoned. The crew, especially London, had become incapacitated after being stricken with a variety of tropical ailments.

Still, even while at sea, London wrote when time permitted. The great distance from home and the fresh salt air ignited his creativity; among other things, he wrote *Martin Eden*, one of his crowning achievements, which was completed at Papeete, Tahiti. After completing the manuscript, he described the novel in a letter to a friend as "an attack upon the bourgeoisie and all that the bourgeoisie stand for. It will not make me any friends." The cruise of the *Snark* had not been a complete failure. London managed to say some things he had to say.

When the author and his wife returned to Glen Ellen, tired and disappointed, in July 1909, the Ranch was a welcome sight. The temperate California summer served as a soothing antidote to the distress of the tropical maladies contracted during the *Snark* voyage. London resumed his daily writing routine, and also concentrated on expanding the boundaries of his "Beauty Ranch," as it was called, until it eventually covered nearly 1,400 acres.

A growing attachment to the Ranch also inspired London to experiment with themes closer to home—themes that departed sharply from his frequent use of the Darwinian theory of the "survival of the fittest." As a result, his return to the land is mirrored in his later writing, particularly within *Burning Daylight* and *The Valley of the Moon*.

He began to put more and more of his time and energy into the development of the Ranch, which, in turn, meant that he had to keep up his frenetic writing pace to satisfy creditors. In fact, during the next seven years, he published twenty-three volumes (seven additional books were published posthumously)—sociological collections, science fiction, tales of the South Seas, travelogues, his agrarian novels, and short stories covering a multitude of themes. Yet, the productivity and success of his writing began to be marred by personal loss and grief.

London still wanted to be a father, and he desperately wanted a son to carry on the family name. He saw his daughters periodically in Oakland and took them on outings in the community and across the Bay in San Francisco. But Bessie never allowed the girls to visit him at the Beauty Ranch.

In 1910, Charmian gave birth to a girl named Joy, but the infant died shortly afterward. Two years later, a second pregnancy ended in a miscarriage. By then, Charmian was over forty years old. London seemed destined to be denied the son he had hoped for.

During this time, he also planned and supervised the construction of his stone and redwood mansion, Wolf House. But late one August evening in 1913, two weeks before the Londons planned to move in, it was destroyed by fire of unknown origin. This was a terrible blow, and it seems as though a part of London's vigor and spirit was consumed by the flames as well. In addition, his health began to decline dramatically. He ignored his doctors' advice, failed to follow a prescribed diet, and this, in conjunction with his drinking and intake of drugs to combat uremia, was more than his body could tolerate. One has only to look at photographs of the author at this time to see that he had aged prematurely and was sick and depressed.

In 1914, while covering the Mexican Revolution in Vera Cruz for *Collier's Magazine*, he contracted a severe case of dysentery. Valiant attempts to improve his health by extended vacations in Hawaii in 1915 and 1916 did little to regenerate the once robust London, but ill as he was, and often weary of writing, London's mind was never dormant. An avid reader all his life, he had, during these last few years, become fascinated with the works of Freud and Jung. Indeed, one can see evidence of their influence in his use of myth and archetypal symbolism in several of his Hawaiian tales. Only a few months before he died, he told Charmian, "I tell you I am standing on the edge of a world so new, so terrible, so wonderful, that I am almost afraid to look over into it." Had he been granted another ten or twenty years of life, who can say what new regions of thought he might have explored and left as part of his literary legacy.

The cause of Jack London's death has been shrouded in mystery and controversy for years. Symbolically, the beginning of the end came when he resigned from the Socialist Party in March 1916 "because of its lack of fire and fight, and its loss of emphasis on the class struggle." Eight months later, on November 22, he died in his cottage on the Beauty Ranch. He was forty years old. The four attending physicians subsequently issued a bulletin attributing the cause of his death to a "gastrointestinal type of uraemia." There have been some who have speculated that he took his own life. More recent evidence by scholars and biographers indicates that in all probability, London died of natural causes, complicated by uremic poisoning, hastened by an unintentional overdose of prescribed morphine and atrophine sulphates.

As London wished, his funeral service was simple. After cremation in Oakland, his ashes were returned and interred on a wooded knoll on the Beauty Ranch just a short distance from the stone ruins of Wolf House. A huge boulder, too large for use in the construction of London's home, was placed over his grave. Only a few close relatives and friends, and several ranch hands attended the ceremony.

Today more than 100,000 people annually pay homage to the author at the Jack London State Historical Park in Glen Ellen, located forty miles north of San Francisco. There, visitors can see his grave and the cottage in which he lived and died, visit the ruins of Wolf House, wander along trails that lead up to Sonoma Mountain (offering a magnificent view of the Valley of the Moon), and browse through the House of Happy Walls, which contains a remarkable display of London memorabilia. Incredibly, except for a few new buildings and paved roads in the area, not much has changed since the days when London himself could be seen sitting in his horse-drawn rig, reins in hand, bouncing down the Ranch road into the village.

Though he has been gone now for more than two generations, London's vivid, often picturesque writings about California remain a vital part of the state's literary history. The full measure of his effort, which captured a panorama of this remarkable land of contrasts from 1891 to 1916, can be judged by London's lasting and versal appeal. Certainly a large part of this appeal can be attributed to his enthusiasm and genuine love of, life. Even before he had achieved literary fame with the publication of his classic, *The Call of the Wild* in 1903 (which begins on a ranch in California's "sun-kissed Santa Clara Valley"), his life had been as active and varied in worldly experiences as to be the envy of any armchair adventurer. Widely read, his work continues to be reprinted because he appeals to the youth, romance, and poetry inherent in all of us. Recognized the world over, Jack London remains a literary phenomenon of the last vestige of the Western frontier, and more uniquely, a Californian at heart.

Sal Noto
Cupertino, California
1985

"I realize that much of California's romance is passing away, and I intend to see to it that I, at least, shall preserve as much of that romance as is possible for me."

—*Jack London to a Sacramento reporter, 1910*

1.

The Golden Poppy

"The Golden Poppy" is one of the more unusual narratives Jack London wrote. The story reads as a rather whimsical commentary on the human condition—in this instance, property encroachment—embracing London's concern for his immediate environment and the American dream of "the pursuit of happiness."

When London wrote it, he was renting a rustic home, "The Bungalow," which was perched on the poppy-clad slopes of the Piedmont Hills just above Oakland. There, with his wife and child, he enjoyed a panoramic view of San Francisco Bay, and settled into a highly disciplined routine as a professional writer. Producing a steady 1,000 words per day, six days per week, he was deluging editors across the country with stories and articles. So it is not surprising that he considered some of his experiences on the very locale in which he lived as suitable material for his pen.

London claimed that "The Golden Poppy" was, in fact, "a true narrative." Anxious to break into print, he took a mundane and capricious incident from his daily life and wrote a memorable sketch.

"The Bungalow" on Blair Avenue overlooking San Francisco Bay. It was while living here that London wrote "The Golden Poppy" during the spring of 1902.

THE GOLDEN POPPY

I HAVE A POPPY FIELD. THAT IS, BY THE GRACE OF GOD AND the good-nature of editors, I am enabled to place each month divers gold pieces into a clerical gentleman's hands, and in return for said gold pieces I am each month reinvested with certain proprietary rights in a poppy field. This field blazes on the rim of the Piedmont Hills. Beneath lies all the world. In the distance, across the silver sweep of bay, San Francisco smokes on her many hills like a second Rome. Not far away, Mount Tamalpais thrusts a rugged shoulder into the sky; and midway between is the Golden Gate, where sea mists love to linger. From the poppy field we often see the shimmering blue of the Pacific beyond, and the busy ships that go forever out and in.

"We shall have great joy in our poppy field," said Bess. "Yes," said I; "how the poor city folk will envy when they come to see us, and how we will make all well again when we send them off with great golden armfuls!"

"But those things will have to come down," I added, pointing to numerous obtrusive notices (relics of the last tenant) displayed conspicuously along the boundaries, and bearing, each and all, this legend:—

"Private Grounds. No Trespassing."

"Why should we refuse the poor city folk a ramble over our field, because, forsooth, they have not the advantage of our acquaintance?"

"How I abhor such things," said Bess; "the arrogant symbols of power."

"They disgrace human nature," said I.

"They shame the generous landscape," she said, "and they are abominable."

"Piggish!" quoth I, hotly. "Down with them!"

We looked forward to the coming of the poppies, did Bess and I, looked forward as only creatures of the city may look who have been long denied. I have forgotten to mention the existence of a house

5

above the poppy field, a squat and wandering bungalow in which we had elected to forsake town traditions and live in fresher and more vigorous ways. The first poppies came, orange-yellow and golden in the standing grain, and we went about gleefully, as though drunken with their wine, and told each other that the poppies were there. We laughed at unexpected moments, in the midst of silences, and at times grew ashamed and stole forth secretly to gaze upon our treasury. But when the great wave of poppy-flame finally spilled itself down the field, we shouted aloud, and danced, and clapped our hands, freely and frankly mad.

And then came the Goths. My face was in a lather, the time of the first invasion, and I suspended my razor in mid-air to gaze out on my beloved field. At the far end I saw a little girl and a little boy, their arms filled with yellow spoil. Ah, thought I, an unwonted benevolence burgeoning, what a delight to me is their delight! It is sweet that children should pick poppies in my field. All summer shall they pick poppies in my field. But they must be little children, I added as an afterthought, and they must pick from the lower end—this last prompted by a glance at the great golden fellows nodding in the wheat beneath my window. Then the razor descended. Shaving was always an absorbing task, and I did not glance out of the window again until the operation was completed. And then I was bewildered. Surely this was not my poppy field. No—and yes, for there were the tall pines clustering austerely together on one side, the magnolia tree burdened with bloom, and the Japanese quinces splashing the driveway hedge with blood. Yes, it was the field, but no wave of poppy-flame spilled down it, nor did the great golden fellows nod in the wheat beneath my window. I rushed into a jacket and out of the house. In the far distance were disappearing two huge balls of color, orange and yellow, for all the world like perambulating poppies of cyclopean breed.

"Johnny," said I to the nine-year-old son of my sister, "Johnny, whenever little girls come into our field to pick poppies, you must go down to them, and in a very quiet and gentlemanly manner, tell them it is not allowed."

Warm days came, and the sun drew another blaze from the free-bosomed earth. Whereupon a neighbor's little girl, at the behest of her mother, duly craved and received permission from Bess to gather a few poppies for decorative purposes. But of this I was uninformed, and when I descried her in the midst of the field I waved my arms like a semaphore against the sky.

"Little girl!" called I. "Little girl!"

The little girl's legs blurred the landscape as she fled, and in high elation I sought Bess to tell of the potency of my voice. Nobly she came to the rescue, departing forthwith on an expedition of conciliation and explanation to the little girl's mother. But to this day the little girl seeks cover at sight of me, and I know the mother will never be as cordial as she would otherwise have been.

Came dark, overcast days, stiff, driving winds and pelting rains, day on day, without end, and the city folk cowered in their dwelling-places like flood-beset rats; and like rats, half-drowned and gasping, when the weather cleared they crawled out and up the green Piedmont slopes to bask in the blessed sunshine. And they invaded my field in swarms and droves, crushing the sweet wheat into the earth and with lustful hands ripping the poppies out by the roots.

"I shall put up the warnings against trespassing," I said.

"Yes," said Bess, with a sigh. "I'm afraid it is necessary."

The day was yet young when she sighed again: "I'm afraid, O Man, that your signs are of no avail. People have forgotten how to read, these days."

I went out on the porch. A city nymph, in cool summer gown and picture hat, paused before one of my newly reared warnings and read it through with care. Profound deliberation characterized her movements. She was statuesquely tall, but with a toss of the head and a flirt of the skirt she dropped on hands and knees, crawled under the fence, and came to her feet on the inside with poppies in both her hands. I walked down the drive and talked ethically to her, and she went away. Then I put up more signs.

At one time, years ago, these hills were carpeted with poppies. As between the destructive forces and the will "to live," the poppies maintained an equilibrium with their environment. But the city folk constituted a new and terrible destructive force, the equilibrium was overthrown, and the poppies well-nigh perished. Since the city folk plucked those with the longest stems and biggest bowls, and since it is the law of kind to procreate kind, the long-stemmed, big-bowled poppies failed to go to seed, and a stunted, short-stemmed variety remained to the hills. And not only was it stunted and short-stemmed, but sparsely distributed as well. Each day and every day, for years and years, the city folk swarmed over the Piedmont Hills, and only here and there did the genius of the race survive in the form of miserable little flowers, close-clinging and quick-blooming, like children of the slums dragged hastily and precariously through youth to a shrivelled and futile maturity.

On the other hand, the poppies had prospered in my field; and not only had they been sheltered from the barbarians, but also from the birds. Long ago the field was sown in wheat, which went to seed

7

unharvested each year, and in the cool depths of which the poppy seeds were hidden from the keen-eyed songsters. And, further, climbing after the sun through the wheat stalks, the poppies grew taller and taller and more royal even than the primordial ones of the open.

So the city folk, gazing from the bare hills to my blazing, burning field, were sorely tempted, and, it must be told, as sorely fell. But no sorer was their fall than that of my beloved poppies. Where the grain holds the dew and takes the bite from the sun the soil is moist, and in such soil it is easier to pull the poppies out by the roots than to break the stalk. Now the city folk, like other folk, are inclined to move along the line of least resistance, and for each flower they gathered, there were also gathered many crisp-rolled buds and with them all the possibilities and future beauties of the plant for all time to come.

One of the city folk, a middle-aged gentleman, with white hands and shifty eyes, especially made life interesting for me. We called him the "Repeater," what of his ways. When from the porch we implored him to desist, he was wont slowly and casually to direct his steps toward the fence, simulating finely the actions of a man who had not heard, but whose walk, instead, had terminated of itself or of his own volition. To heighten this effect, now and again, still casually and carelessly, he would stoop and pluck another poppy. Thus did he deceitfully save himself the indignity of being put out, and rob us of the satisfaction of putting him out, but he came, and he came often, each time getting away with an able-bodied man's share of plunder.

It is not good to be of the city folk. Of this I am convinced. There is something in the mode of life that breeds an alarming condition of blindness and deafness, or so it seems with the city folk that come to my poppy field. Of the many to whom I have talked ethically not one has been found who ever saw the warnings so conspicuously displayed, while of those called out to from the porch, possibly one in fifty has heard. Also, I have discovered that the relation of city folk to country flowers is quite analogous to that of a starving man to food. No more than the starving man realizes that five pounds of meat is not so good as an ounce, do they realize that five hundred poppies crushed and bunched are less beautiful than two or three in a free cluster, where the green leaves and golden bowls may expand to their full loveliness.

Less forgivable than the unaesthetic are the mercenary. Hordes of young rascals plunder me and rob the future that they may stand on street corners and retail "California poppies, only five cents a bunch!" In spite of my precautions some of them made a dollar a day out of my field. One horde do I remember with keen regret. Reconnoitring for a possible dog, they applied at the kitchen door for "a drink of water, please." While they drank they were besought not to pick any flowers. They nodded, wiped their mouths, and proceeded to take themselves off by the side of the bungalow. They smote the poppy field beneath my windows, spread out fan-shaped six wide, picking with both hands, and ripped a swath of destruction through the very heart of the field. No cyclone travelled faster or destroyed more completely. I shouted after them, but they sped on the wings of the wind, great regal poppies, broken-stalked and mangled, trailing after them or cluttering their wake—the most highhanded act of piracy, I am confident, ever committed off the high seas.

One day I went a-fishing, and on that day a woman entered the field. Appeals and remonstrances from the porch having no effect upon her, Bess despatched a little girl to beg of her to pick no more poppies. The woman calmly went on picking. Then Bess herself went down through the heat of the day. But the woman went on picking, and while she picked she discussed property and proprietary rights, denying Bess's sovereignty until deeds and documents should be produced in proof thereof. And all the time she went on picking, never once overlooking her hand. She was a large woman, belligerent of aspect, and Bess was only a woman and not prone to fisticuffs. So the invader picked until she could pick no more, said "Good-day," and sailed majestically away.

"People have really grown worse in the last several years, I think," said Bess to me in a tired sort of voice that night, as we sat in the library after dinner.

Next day I was inclined to agree with her. "There's a woman and a little girl heading straight for the poppies," said May, a maid about the bungalow. I went out on the porch and waited their advent. They plunged through the pine trees and into the fields, and as the roots of the first poppies were pulled I called to them. They were about a hundred feet away. The woman and the little girl turned to the sound of my voice and looked at me. "Please do not pick the poppies," I pleaded. They pondered this for a minute; then the woman said something in an undertone to the little girl, and both backs jackknifed as the slaughter recommenced. I shouted, but they had become suddenly deaf. I screamed, and so fiercely that the little girl wavered dubiously. And while the woman went on picking I could hear her in low tones heartening the little girl.

I recollected a siren whistle with which I was wont to summon

Johnny, the son of my sister. It was a fearsome thing, of a kind to wake the dead, and I blew and blew, but the jack-knifed backs never unclasped. I do not mind with men, but I have never particularly favored physical encounters with women; yet this woman, who encouraged a little girl in iniquity, tempted me.

I went into the bungalow and fetched my rifle. Flourishing it in a sanguinary manner and scowling fearsomely, I charged upon the invaders. The little girl fled, screaming, to the shelter of the pines, but the woman calmly went on picking. She took not the least notice. I had expected her to run at sight of me, and it was embarrassing. There was I, charging down the field like a wild bull upon a woman who would not get out of the way. I could only slow down, supremely conscious of how ridiculous it all was. At a distance of ten feet she straightened up and deigned to look at me. I came to a halt and blushed to the roots of my hair. Perhaps I really did frighten her (I sometimes try to persuade myself that this is so), or perhaps she took pity on me; but, at any rate, she stalked out of my field with great composure, nay, majesty, her arms brimming with orange and gold.

Nevertheless, thenceforward I saved my lungs and flourished my rifle. Also, I made fresh generalizations. To commit robbery women take advantage of their sex. Men have more respect for property than women. Men are less insistent in crime than women. And women are less afraid of guns than men. Likewise, we conquer the earth in hazard and battle by the virtues of our mothers. We are a race of land-robbers and sea-robbers, we Anglo-Saxons, and small wonder, when we suckle at the breasts of a breed of women such as maraud my poppy field.

Still the pillage went on. Sirens and gun-flourishings were without avail. The city folk were great of heart and undismayed, and I noted the habit of "repeating" was becoming general. What booted it how often they were driven forth if each time they were permitted to carry away their ill-gotten plunder? When one has turned the same person away twice and thrice an emotion arises somewhat akin to homicide. And when one has once become conscious of this sanguinary feeling his whole destiny seems to grip hold of him and drag him into the abyss. More than once I found myself unconsciously pulling the rifle into position to get a sight on the miserable trespassers. In my sleep I slew them in manifold ways and threw their carcasses into the reservoir. Each day the temptation to shoot them in the legs became more luring, and every day I felt my fate calling to me imperiously. Visions of the gallows rose up before me, and with the hemp about my neck I saw stretched out the pitiless future of my children, dark with disgrace and shame. I became afraid of myself, and Bess went about with anxious face, privily beseeching my friends to entice me into taking a vacation. Then, and at the last gasp, came the thought that saved me: *Why not confiscate?* If their forays were bootless, in the nature of things their forays would cease.

The first to enter my field thereafter was a man. I was waiting for him—And, oh joy! it was the "Repeater" himself, smugly complacent with knowledge of past success. I dropped the rifle negligently across the hollow of my arm and went down to him.

"I am sorry to trouble you for those poppies," I said in my oiliest tones; "but really, you know, I must have them."

He regarded me speechlessly. It must have made a great picture. It surely was dramatic. With the rifle across my arm and my suave request still ringing in my ears, I felt like Black Bart, and Jesse James, and Jack Shepard, and Robin Hood, and whole generations of highwaymen.

"Come, come," I said, a little sharply and in what I imagined was the true fashion; "I am sorry to inconvenience you, believe me, but I must have those poppies."

I absently shifted the gun and smiled. That fetched him. Without a word he passed them over and turned his toes toward the fence, but no longer casual and careless was his carriage, nor did he stoop to pick the occasional poppy by the way. That was the last of the "Repeater." I could see by his eyes that he did not like me, and his back reproached me all the way down the field and out of sight.

From that day the bungalow has been flooded with poppies. Every vase and earthen jar is filled with them. They blaze on every mantel and run riot through all the rooms. I present them to my friends in huge bunches, and still the kind city folk come and gather more for me. "Sit down for a moment," I say to the departing guest. And there we sit in the shade of the porch while aspiring city creatures pluck my poppies and sweat under the brazen sun. And when their arms are sufficiently weighted with my yellow glories, I go down with the rifle over my arm and disburden them. Thus have I become convinced that every situation has its compensations.

Confiscation was successful, so far as it went; but I had forgotten one thing; namely, the vast number of the city folk. Though the old transgressors came no more, new ones arrived every day, and I found myself confronted with the titanic task of educating a whole cityful to the inexpediency of raiding my poppy field. During the process of disburdening them I was accustomed to explaining my side of the case, but I soon gave this over. It was a waste of breath. They could not understand. To one lady, who insinuated that I was miserly, I said:

"My dear madam, no hardship is worked upon you. Had I not

been parsimonious yesterday and the day before, these poppies would have been picked by the city hordes of that day and the day before, and your eyes, which to-day have discovered this field, would have beheld no poppies at all. The poppies you may not pick to-day are the poppies I did not permit to be picked yesterday and the day before. Therefore, believe me, you are denied nothing."

"But the poppies are here to-day," she said, glaring carnivorously upon their glow and splendor.

"I will pay you for them," said a gentleman, at another time. (I had just relieved him of an armful.) I felt a sudden shame, I know not why, unless it be that his words had just made clear to me that a monetary as well as an aesthetic value was attached to my flowers. The apparent sordidness of my position overwhelmed me, and I said weakly: "I do not sell my poppies. You may have what you have picked." But before the week was out I confronted the same gentleman again. "I will pay you for them." he said. "Yes," I said, "you may pay me for them. Twenty dollars, please." He gasped, looked at me searchingly, gasped again, and silently and sadly put the poppies down. But it remained, as usual, for a woman to attain the sheerest pitch of audacity. When I declined payment and demanded my plucked beauties, she refused to give them up. "I picked these poppies," she said, "and my time is worth money. When you have paid me for my time you may have them." Her cheeks flamed rebellion, and her face, withal a pretty one, was set and determined. Now, I was a man of the hill tribes, and she a mere woman of the city folk, and though it is not my inclination to enter into details, it is my pleasure to state that that bunch of poppies subsequently glorified the bungalow and that the woman departed to the city unpaid. Anyway, they were my poppies.

"They are God's poppies," said the Radiant Young Radical, democratically shocked at sight of me turning city folk out of my field. And for two weeks she hated me with a deathless hatred. I sought her out and explained. I explained at length. I told the story of the poppy as Maeterlink has told the life of the bee. I treated the question biologically, psychologically, and sociologically. I discussed it ethically and aesthetically. I grew warm over it, and impassioned; and when I had done, she professed conversion, but in my heart of hearts I knew it to be compassion.

I fled to other friends for consolation. I retold the story of the poppy. They did not appear supremely interested. I grew excited. They were surprised and pained. They looked at me curiously. "It ill-befits your dignity to squabble over poppies," they said. "It is unbecoming."

I fled away to yet other friends. I sought vindication. The thing had become vital, and I needs must put myself right. I felt called upon to explain, though well knowing that he who explains is lost. I told the story of the poppy over again. I went into the minutest details. I added to it, and expanded. I talked myself hoarse, and when I could talk no more they looked bored. Also, they said insipid things, and soothful things, and things concerning other things, and not at all to the point. I was consumed with anger, and there and then I renounced them all.

At the bungalow I lie in wait for chance visitors. Craftily I broach the subject, watching their faces closely the while to detect first signs of disapprobation, whereupon I empty long-stored vials of wrath upon their heads. I wrangle for hours with whomsoever does not say I am right. I am become like Guy de Maupassant's old man who picked up a piece of string. I am incessantly explaining, and nobody will understand. I have become more brusque in my treatment of the predatory city folk. No longer do I take delight in their disburdenment, for it has become an onerous duty, a wearisome and distasteful task. My friends look askance and murmur pityingly on the side when we meet in the city. They rarely come to see me now. They are afraid. I am an embittered and disappointed man, and all the light seems to have gone out of my life and into my blazing field. So one pays for things.

George Sterling, London's closest friend and the prototype for the poet, Brissenden, in *Martin Eden*.

2.

In the Piedmont Hills
and
Intellectual Reveries
in San Francisco

SELECTIONS FROM MARTIN EDEN

In August 1908, one month prior to the serialization of this auto-biographical novel in Pacific Monthly magazine, the editors announced that "Martin Eden . . . possesses more of the fascination and virility, grips the imagination and the sympathies more keenly, and imparts more of courage than any book produced in years." The readers were not to be disappointed, yet London himself was less certain about the merits of the story. Earlier, in a letter to the same editors, he wrote, "I don't know what you will think of this novel; I do not know what to think of it myself. But at any rate you will find it entirely different from anything else I have done."

Perhaps London had put more of himself into the novel than he realized, and couldn't "see the forest for the trees." Yet several years later he declared, "I was Martin Eden." Evidently the passage of time gave the author the objectivity he needed to come to terms with such a personal book. Without question there is more of Jack London within Martin Eden than in anything else he ever wrote.

The first selection (from Chapter 21) finds the youthful Martin Eden—a struggling writer, idealistic, full of hope—and Ruth Morse, a refined and well-educated young lady he adores, confessing their love for each other on a hillside overlooking San Francisco Bay.

Later, in the second selection (from Chapter 36), Martin is on the threshold of literary success. In this scene, Brissenden, his poet friend (based on London's close friend George Sterling), introduces him to a group of intellectuals who live bohemian-style in the area of San Francisco south of Market Street. Here he is inspired by stimulating discussions on philosophical and political topics that he is just beginning to comprehend and appreciate.

Parts of this scene are certainly reminiscent of London's own Wednesday night gatherings with his artist and writer friends at his home in the Piedmont Hills during the early 1900s.

IN THE PIEDMONT HILLS

CAME A BEAUTIFUL FALL DAY, WARM AND LANGUID, PAL-
pitant with the hush of the changing season, a California Indian
summer day, with hazy sun and wandering wisps of breeze that did
not stir the slumber of the air. Filmy purple mists, that were not
vapors but fabrics woven of color, hid in the recesses of the hills.
San Francisco lay like a blur of smoke upon her heights. The inter-
vening bay was a dull sheen of molten metal, whereon sailing craft
lay motionless or drifted with the lazy tide. Far Tamalpais, barely
seen in the silver haze, bulked hugely by the Golden Gate, the latter
a pale gold pathway under the westering sun. Beyond, the Pacific,
dim and vast, was raising on its sky-line tumbled cloud-masses that
swept landward, giving warning of the first blustering breath of
winter.

The erasure of summer was at hand. Yet summer lingered, fading
and fainting among her hills, deepening the purple of her valleys,
spinning a shroud of haze from waning powers and sated raptures,
dying with the calm content of having lived and lived well. And
among the hills, on their favorite knoll, Martin and Ruth sat side by
side, their heads bent over the same pages, he reading aloud from
the love-sonnets of the woman who had loved Browning as it is given
to few men to be loved.

But the reading languished. The spell of passing beauty all about
them was too strong. The golden year was dying as it had lived, a
beautiful and unrepentant voluptuary, and reminiscent rapture and
content freighted heavily the air. It entered into them, dreamy and
languorous, weakening the fibres of resolution, suffusing the face of
morality, or of judgment, with haze and purple mist. Martin felt
tender and melting, and from time to time warm glows passed over
him. His head was very near to hers, and when wandering phan-
toms of breeze stirred her hair so that it touched his face, the printed
pages swam before his eyes.

"I don't believe you know a word of what you are reading," she
said once when he had lost his place.

He looked at her with burning eyes, and was on the verge of becoming awkward, when a retort came to his lips.

"I don't believe you know either. What was the last sonnet about?"

17

"I don't know," she laughed frankly. "I've already forgotten. Don't let us read any more. The day is too beautiful."

"It will be our last in the hills for some time," he announced gravely. "There's a storm gathering out there on the sea-rim."

The book slipped from his hands to the ground, and they sat idly and silently, gazing out over the dreamy bay with eyes that dreamed and did not see. Ruth glanced sidewise at his neck. She did not lean toward him. She was drawn by some force outside of herself and stronger than gravitation, strong as destiny. It was only an inch to lean, and it was accomplished without volition on her part. Her shoulder touched his as lightly as a butterfly touches a flower, and just as lightly was the counter-pressure. She felt his shoulder press hers, and a tremor run through him. Then was the time for her to draw back. But she had become an automaton. Her actions had passed beyond the control of her will—she never thought of control or will in the delicious madness that was upon her. His arm began to steal behind her and around her. She waited its slow progress in a torment of delight. She waited, she knew not for what, panting, with dry, burning lips, a leaping pulse, and a fever of expectancy in all her blood. The girdling arm lifted higher and drew her toward him, drew her slowly and caressingly. She could wait no longer. With a tired sigh, and with an impulsive movement all her own, unpremeditated, spasmodic, she rested her head upon his breast. His head bent over swiftly, and, as his lips approached, hers flew to meet them.

This must be love, she thought, in the one rational moment that was vouchsafed her. If it was not love, it was too shameful. It could be nothing else than love. She loved the man whose arms were around her and whose lips were pressed to hers. She pressed more tightly to him, with a snuggling movement of her body. And a moment later, tearing herself half out of his embrace, suddenly and exultantly she reached up and placed both hands upon Martin Eden's sunburnt neck. So exquisite was the pang of love and desire fulfilled that she uttered a low moan, relaxed her hands, and lay half-swooning in his arms.

Not a word had been spoken, and not a word was spoken for a long time. Twice he bent and kissed her, and each time her lips met his shyly and her body made its happy, nestling movement. She clung to him, unable to release herself, and he sat, half supporting her in his arms, as he gazed with unseeing eyes at the blur of the great city across the bay. For once there were no visions in his brain. Only colors and lights and glows pulsed there, warm as the day and warm as his love. He bent over her. She was speaking.

"When did you love me?" she whispered.

"From the first, the very first, the first moment I laid eyes on you, I was mad for love of you then, and in all the time that has passed since then I have only grown the madder. I am maddest, now, dear. I am almost a lunatic, my head is so turned with joy."

"I am glad I am a woman, Martin—dear," she said, after a long sigh.

He crushed her in his arms again and again, and then asked:—

"And you? When did you first know?"

"Oh, I knew it all the time, almost from the first."

"And I have been as blind as a bat!" he cried, a ring of vexation in his voice. "I never dreamed it until just now, when I—when I kissed you."

"I didn't mean that." She drew herself partly away and looked at him. "I meant I knew you loved me almost from the first."

"And you?" he demanded.

"It came to me suddenly." She was speaking very slowly, her eyes warm and fluttery and melting, a soft flush on her cheeks that did not go away. "I never knew until just now when—you put your arms around me. And I never expected to marry you, Martin, not until just now. How did you make me love you?"

"I don't know," he laughed, "unless just by loving you, for I loved you hard enough to melt the heart of a stone, much less the heart of the living, breathing woman you are."

"This is so different from what I thought love would be," she announced irrelevantly.

"What did you think it would be like?"

"I didn't think it would be like this." She was looking into his eyes at the moment, but her own dropped as she continued, "You see, I didn't know what this was like."

He offered to draw her toward him again, but it was no more than a tentative muscular movement of the girdling arm, for he feared that he might be greedy. Then he felt her body yielding, and once again she was close in his arms and lips were pressed on lips.

"What will my people say?" she queried, with sudden apprehension, in one of the pauses.

"I don't know. We can find out very easily any time we are so minded."

"But if mamma objects? I am sure I am afraid to tell her."

"Let me tell her," he volunteered valiantly. "I think your mother does not like me, but I can win her around. A fellow who can win you can win anything. And if we don't—"

"Yes?"

"Why, we'll have each other. But there's no danger of not winning your mother to our marriage. She loves you too well."

19

"I should not like to break her heart," Ruth said pensively.

He felt like assuring her that mothers' hearts were not so easily broken, but instead he said, "And love is the greatest thing in the world."

"Do you know, Martin, you sometimes frighten me. I am frightened now, when I think of you and of what you have been. You must be very, very good to me. Remember, after all, that I am only a child. I never loved before."

"Nor I. We are both children together. And we are fortunate above most, for we have found our first love in each other."

"But that is impossible!" she cried, withdrawing herself from his arms with a swift, passionate movement. "Impossible for you. You have been a sailor, and sailors, I have heard, are—are—"

Her voice faltered and died away.

"Are addicted to having a wife in every port?" he suggested. "Is that what you mean?"

"Yes," she answered in a low voice.

"But that is not love." He spoke authoritatively. "I have been in many ports, but I never knew a passing touch of love until I saw you that first night. Do you know, when I said good night and went away, I was almost arrested."

"Arrested?"

"Yes. The policeman thought I was drunk; and I was, too—with love for you."

"But you said we were children, and I said it was impossible, for you, and we have strayed away from the point."

"I said that I never loved anybody but you," he replied. "You are my first, my very first."

"And yet you have been a sailor," she objected.

"But that doesn't prevent me from loving you the first."

"And there have been women—other women—oh!"

And to Martin Eden's supreme surprise, she burst into a storm of tears that took more kisses than one and many caresses to drive away. And all the while there was running through his head Kipling's line: "And the Colonel's lady and Judy O'Grady are sisters under their skins." It was true, he decided; though the novels he had read had led him to believe otherwise. His idea, for which the novels were responsible, had been that only formal proposals obtained in the upper classes. It was all right enough, down whence he had come, for youths and maidens to win each other by contact; but for the exalted personages up above on the heights to make love in similar fashion had seemed unthinkable. Yet the novels were wrong. Here was a proof of it. The same pressures and caresses, unaccompanied by speech, that were efficacious with the girls of the working-class, were equally efficacious with the girls above the working-class. They were all of the same flesh, after all, sisters under their skins; and he might have known as much himself had he remembered his Spencer. As he held Ruth in his arms and soothed her, he took great consolation in the thought that the Colonel's lady and Judy O'Grady were pretty much alike under their skins. It brought Ruth closer to him, made her possible. Her dear flesh was as anybody's flesh, as his flesh. There was no bar to their marriage. Class difference was the only difference, and class was extrinsic. It could be shaken off. A slave, he had read, had risen to the Roman purple. That being so, then he could rise to Ruth. Under her purity, and saintliness, and culture, and ethereal beauty of soul, she was, in things fundamentally human, just like Lizzie Connolly and all Lizzie Connollys. All that was possible of them was possible of her. She could love, and hate, maybe have hysterics; and she could certainly be jealous, as she was jealous now, uttering her last sobs in his arms.

"Besides, I am older than you," she remarked suddenly, opening her eyes and looking up at him, "three years older."

"Hush, you are only a child, and I am forty years older than you, in experience," was his answer.

In truth, they were children together, so far as love was concerned, and they were as naïve and immature in the expression of their love as a pair of children, and this despite the fact that she was crammed with a university education and that his head was full of scientific philosophy and the hard facts of life.

They sat on through the passing glory of the day, talking as lovers are prone to talk, marvelling at the wonder of love and at destiny that had flung them so strangely together, and dogmatically believing that they loved to a degree never attained by lovers before. And they returned insistently, again and again, to a rehearsal of their first impressions of each other and to hopeless attempts to analyze just precisely what they felt for each other and how much there was of it.

The cloud-masses on the western horizon received the descending sun, and the circle of the sky turned to rose, while the zenith glowed with the same warm color. The rosy light was all about them, flooding over them, as she sang, "Good-by, Sweet Day." She sang softly, leaning in the cradle of his arms, her hands in his, their hearts in each other's hands.

INTELLECTUAL REVERIES
IN SAN FRANCISCO

"COME ON—I'LL SHOW YOU THE REAL DIRT," BRISSENDEN said to him, one evening in January.

They had dined together in San Francisco, and were at the Ferry Building, returning to Oakland, when the whim came to him to show Martin the "real dirt." He turned and fled across the water-front, a meagre shadow in a flapping overcoat, with Martin straining to keep up with him. At a wholesale liquor store he bought two gallon-demijohns of old port, and with one in each hand boarded a Mission Street car, Martin at his heels burdened with several quart-bottles of whiskey.

If Ruth could see me now, was his thought, while he wondered as to what constituted the real dirt.

"Maybe nobody will be there," Brissenden said, when they dismounted and plunged off to the right into the heart of the working-class ghetto, south of Market Street. "In which case you'll miss what you've been looking for so long."

"And what the deuce is that?" Martin asked.

"Men, intelligent men, and not the gibbering nonentities I found you consorting with in that trader's den. You read the books and you found yourself all alone. Well, I'm going to show you to-night some other men who've read the books, so that you won't be lonely any more.

"Not that I bother my head about their everlasting discussions," he said at the end of a block. "I'm not interested in book philosophy. But you'll find these fellows intelligences and not bourgeois swine. But watch out, they'll talk an arm off of you on any subject under the sun.

"Hope Norton's there," he panted a little later, resisting Martin's effort to relieve him of the two demijohns. "Norton's an idealist—a Harvard man. Prodigious memory. Idealism led him to philosophic anarchy, and his family threw him off. Father's a railroad president and many times millionaire, but the son's starving in 'Frisco, editing an anarchist sheet for twenty-five a month."

Martin was little acquainted in San Francisco, and not at all south of Market; so he had no idea of where he was being led.

"Go ahead," he said; "tell me about them beforehand. What do they do for a living? How do they happen to be here?"

"Hope Hamilton's there." Brissenden paused and rested his hands. "Strawn-Hamilton's his name—hyphenated, you know—comes of old Southern stock. He's a tramp—laziest man I ever knew, though he's clerking, or trying to, in a socialist coöperative store for six dollars a week. But he's a confirmed hobo. Tramped into town. I've seen him sit all day on a bench and never a bite pass his lips, and in the evening, when I invited him to dinner—restaurant two blocks away—have him say, 'Too much trouble, old man. Buy me a package of cigarettes instead.' He was a Spencerian like you till Kreis turned him to materialistic monism. I'll start him on monism if I can. Norton's another monist—only he affirms naught but spirit. He can give Kreis and Hamilton all they want, too."

"Who is Kreis?" Martin asked.

"His rooms we're going to. One time professor—fired from university—usual story. A mind like a steel trap. Makes his living any old way. I know he's been a street fakir when he was down. Unscrupulous. Rob a corpse of a shroud—anything. Difference between him and the bourgeoisie is that he robs without illusion. He'll talk Nietzsche, or Schopenhauer, or Kant, or anything, but the only thing in this world, not excepting Mary, that he really cares for, is his monism. Haeckel is his little tin god. The only way to insult him is to take a slap at Haeckel.

"Here's the hang-out." Brissenden rested his demijohn at the upstairs entrance, preliminary to the climb. It was the usual two-story corner building, with a saloon and grocery underneath. "The gang lives here—got the whole upstairs to themselves. But Kreis is the only one who has two rooms. Come on."

No lights burned in the upper hall, but Brissenden threaded the utter blackness like a familiar ghost. He stopped to speak to Martin.

"There's one fellow—Stevens—a theosophist. Makes a pretty tangle when he gets going. Just now he's dishwasher in a restaurant. Likes a good cigar. I've seen him eat in a ten-cent hash-house and pay fifty cents for the cigar he smoked afterward. I've got a couple in my pocket for him, if he shows up.

"And there's another fellow—Parry—an Australian, a statistician and a sporting encyclopedia. Ask him the grain output of Paraguay for 1903, or the English importation of sheetings into China for 1890, or at what weight Jimmy Britt fought Battling Nelson, or who was welterweight champion of the United States in '68, and you'll get

23

the correct answer with the automatic celerity of a slot-machine. And there's Andy, a stone-mason, has ideas on everything, a good chess-player; and another fellow, Harry, a baker, red hot socialist and strong union man. By the way, you remember the Cooks' and Waiters' strike—Hamilton was the chap who organized that union and pre-cipitated the strike—planned it all out in advance, right here in Kreis's rooms. Did it just for the fun of it, but was too lazy to stay by the union. Yet he could have risen high if he wanted to. There's no end to the possibilities in that man—if he weren't so insupera-bly lazy."

Brissenden advanced through the darkness till a thread of light marked the threshold of a door. A knock and an answer opened it, and Martin found himself shaking hands with Kreis, a handsome brunette man, with dazzling white teeth, a drooping black mus-tache, and large, flashing black eyes. Mary, a matronly young blonde, was washing dishes in the little back room that served for kitchen and dining room. The front room served as bedchamber and living room. Overhead was the week's washing, hanging in festoons so low that Martin did not see at first the two men talking in a corner. They hailed Brissenden and his demijohns with acclamation, and, on being introduced, Martin learned they were Andy and Parry. He joined them and listened attentively to the description of a prize-fight Parry had seen the night before; while Brissenden, in his glory, plunged into the manufacture of a toddy and the serving of wine and whis-key-and-sodas. At his command, "Bring in the clan," Andy de-parted to go the round of the rooms for the lodgers.

"We're lucky that most of them are here," Brissenden whispered to Martin. "There's Norton and Hamilton; come on and meet them. Stevens isn't around, I hear. I'm going to get them started on mon-ism if I can. Wait till they get a few jolts in them and they'll warm up."

At first the conversation was desultory. Nevertheless Martin could not fail to appreciate the keen play of their minds. They were men with opinions, though the opinions often clashed, and, though they were witty and clever, they were not superficial. He swiftly saw, no matter upon what they talked, that each man applied the correla-tion of knowledge and had also a deep-seated and unified concep-tion of society and the Cosmos. Nobody manufactured their opin-ions for them; they were all rebels of one variety or another, and their lips were strangers to platitudes. Never had Martin, at the Morses', heard so amazing a range of topics discussed. There seemed no limit save time to the things they were alive to. The talk wan-dered from Mrs. Humphry Ward's new book to Shaw's latest play, through the future of the drama to reminiscences of Mansfield. They appreciated or sneered at the morning editorials, jumped from labor conditions in New Zealand to Henry James and Brander Matthews, passed on to the German designs in the Far East and the economic aspect of the Yellow Peril, wrangled over the German elections and Bebel's last speech, and settled down to local politics, the latest plans and scandals in the union labor party administration, and the wires that were pulled to bring about the Coast Seamen's strike. Martin was struck by the inside knowledge they possessed. They knew what was never printed in the newspapers—the wires and strings and the hidden hands that made the puppets dance. To Martin's surprise, the girl, Mary, joined in the conversation, displaying an intelligence he had never encountered in the few women he had met. They talked together on Swinburne and Rossetti, after which she led him beyond his depth into the by-paths of French literature. His revenge came when she defended Maeterlinck and he brought into action the carefully-thought-out thesis of "The Shame of the Sun."

Several other men had dropped in, and the air was thick with tobacco smoke, when Brissenden waved the red flag.

"Here's fresh meat for your axe, Kreis," he said; "a rose-white youth with the ardor of a lover for Herbert Spencer. Make a Haeckelite of him—if you can."

Kreis seemed to wake up and flash like some metallic, magnetic thing, while Norton looked at Martin sympathetically, with a sweet, girlish smile, as much as to say that he would be amply protected.

Kreis began directly on Martin, but step by step Norton interfered, until he and Kreis were off and away in a personal battle. Martin listened and fain would have rubbed his eyes. It was impossible that this should be, much less in the labor ghetto south of Market. The books were alive in these men. They talked with fire and enthusiasm, the intellectual stimulant stirring them as he had seen drink and anger stir other men. What he heard was no longer the philosophy of the dry, printed word, written by half-mythical demigods like Kant and Spencer. It was living philosophy, with warm, red blood, incarnated in these two men till its very features worked with excitement. Now and again other men joined in, and all followed the discussion with cigarettes going out in their hands and with alert, intent faces.

Idealism had never attracted Martin, but the exposition it now received at the hands of Norton was a revelation. The logical plausibility of it, that made an appeal to his intellect, seemed missed by Kreis and Hamilton, who sneered at Norton as a metaphysician, and who, in turn, sneered back at them as metaphysicians. *Phenome-*

25

non and *noumenon* were bandied back and forth. They charged him with attempting to explain consciousness by itself. He charged them with word-jugglery, with reasoning from words to theory instead of from facts to theory. At this they were aghast. It was the cardinal tenet of their mode of reasoning to start with facts and to give names to the facts.

When Norton wandered into the intricacies of Kant, Kreis reminded him that all good little German philosophies when they died went to Oxford. A little later Norton reminded them of Hamilton's Law of Parsimony, the application of which they immediately claimed for every reasoning process of theirs. And Martin hugged his knees and exulted in it all. But Norton was no Spencerian, and he, too, strove for Martin's philosophic soul, talking as much at him as to his two opponents.

"You know Berkeley has never been answered," he said, looking directly at Martin. "Herbert Spencer came the nearest, which was not very near. Even the stanchest of Spencer's followers will not go farther. I was reading an essay of Saleeby's the other day, and the best Saleeby could say was that Herbert Spencer *nearly* succeeded in answering Berkeley."

"You know what Hume said?" Hamilton asked. Norton nodded, but Hamilton gave it for the benefit of the rest. "He said that Berkeley's arguments admit of no answer and produce no conviction."

"In his, Hume's, mind," was the reply. "And Hume's mind was the same as yours, with this difference: he was wise enough to admit there was no answering Berkeley."

Norton was sensitive and excitable, though he never lost his head, while Kreis and Hamilton were like a pair of cold-blooded savages, seeking out tender places to prod and poke. As the evening grew late, Norton, smarting under the repeated charges of being a metaphysician, clutching his chair to keep from jumping to his feet, his gray eyes snapping and his girlish face grown harsh and sure, made a grand attack upon their position.

"All right, you Haeckelites, I may reason like a medicine man, but, pray, how do you reason? You have nothing to stand on, you unscientific dogmatists with your positive science which you are always lugging about into places it has no right to be. Long before the school of materialistic monism arose, the ground was removed so that there could be no foundation. Locke was the man, John Locke. Two hundred years ago—more than that, even—in his 'Essay Concerning the Human Understanding,' he proved the non-existence of innate ideas. The best of it is that that is precisely what you claim. To-night, again and again, you have asserted the non-existence of innate ideas.

"And what does that mean? It means that you can never know ultimate reality. Your brains are empty when you are born. Appearances, or phenomena, are all the content your minds can receive from your five senses. Then noumena, which are not in your minds when you are born, have no way of getting in—"

"I deny—" Kreis started to interrupt.

"You wait till I'm done," Norton shouted. "You can know only that much of the play and interplay of force and matter as impinges in one way or another on your senses. You see, I am willing to admit, for the sake of the argument, that matter exists; and what I am about to do is to efface you by your own argument. I can't do it any other way, for you are both congenitally unable to understand a philosophic abstraction.

"And now, what do you know of matter, according to your own positive science? You know it only by its phenomena, its appearances. You are aware only of its changes, or of such changes in it as cause changes in your consciousness. Positive science deals only with phenomena, yet you are foolish enough to strive to be ontologists and to deal with noumena. Yet, by the very definition of positive science, science is concerned only with appearances. As somebody has said, phenomenal knowledge cannot transcend phenomena.

"You cannot answer Berkeley, even if you have annihilated Kant, and yet, perforce, you assume that Berkeley is wrong when you affirm that science proves the non-existence of God, or, as much to the point, the existence of matter.—You know I granted the reality of matter only in order to make myself intelligible to your understanding. Be positive scientists, if you please; but ontology has no place in positive science, so leave it alone. Spencer is right in his agnosticism, but if Spencer—"

But it was time to catch the last ferry-boat for Oakland, and Brissenden and Martin slipped out, leaving Norton still talking and Kreis and Hamilton waiting to pounce on him like a pair of hounds as soon as he finished.

"You have given me a glimpse of fairyland," Martin said on the ferry-boat. "It makes life worth while to meet people like that. My mind is all worked up. I never appreciated idealism before. Yet I can't accept it. I know that I shall always be a realist. I am so made, I guess. But I'd like to have made a reply to Kreis and Hamilton, and I think I'd have had a word or two for Norton. I didn't see that Spencer was damaged any. I'm as excited as a child on its first visit to the circus. I see I must read up some more. I'm going to get hold of Saleeby. I still think Spencer is unassailable, and next time I'm going to take a hand myself."

But Brissenden, breathing painfully, had dropped off to sleep, his chin buried in a scarf and resting on his sunken chest, his body wrapped in the long overcoat and shaking to the vibration of the propellers.

3.

In Search of Eden

SELECTIONS FROM THE VALLEY OF THE MOON

Disillusioned with their working-class existence in Oakland, new-lyweds Billy and Saxon Roberts begin their idyllic search for their "valley of the moon," and a simple and basic life in the country. Young and innocent, they gradually discover each other on a deeper level while hiking through the towns and rural areas of Northern California. In addition, they observe the techniques of successful farming and meet a variety of people along the way—independent and self-sufficient growers, and writers and artists in the bohemian colony at Carmel.

Later, while visiting the river-front village of Collinsville on the banks of the Sacramento, they gain helpful advice from a writer and his wife, Jack and Clara Hastings, who, not so surprisingly, bear a remarkable resemblance to Jack and Charmian London.

In November 1913, shortly after the novel first appeared, a re-view in the New York Sun stated that The Valley of the Moon con-tained "vivid blocks of realism and brilliant scraps of California scenery . . ." Modern-day readers may wonder how the novel has withstood the test of time. Aside from occasional flaws within the narrative (there are snatches of wooden dialogue and typical post-1900 Anglo-Saxon sentiments), The Valley of the Moon remains timely because of its theme of a universal longing to escape from the blight of twentieth-century urbanization and subsequent dehu-manization to a pastoral existence in the country. The selections here, from chapters II, III, and VI, illustrate this theme.

Jack London astride Washoe Ban near the summit of Sonoma Mountain, overloo
ing the Valley of the Moon.

IN SEARCH OF EDEN

IT WAS SUNSET WHEN THEY ENTERED THE LITTLE TOWN OF Niles. Billy, who had been silent for the last half mile, hesitantly ventured a suggestion.

"Say . . . I could put up for a room in the hotel just as well as not. What d'ye think?"

But Saxon shook her head emphatically.

"How long do you think our twenty dollars will last at that rate? Besides, the only way to begin is to begin at the beginning. We didn't plan sleeping in hotels."

"All right," he gave in. "I'm game. I was just thinkin' about you."

"Then you'd better think I'm game, too," she flashed forgivingly. "And now we'll have to see about getting things for supper."

They bought a round steak, potatoes, onions, and a dozen eating apples, then went out from the town to the fringe of trees and brush that advertised a creek. Beside the trees, on a sand bank, they pitched camp. Plenty of dry wood lay about, and Billy whistled genially while he gathered and chopped. Saxon, keen to follow his every mood, was cheered by the atrocious discord on his lips. She smiled to herself as she spread the blankets, with the tarpaulin underneath, for a table, having first removed all twigs from the sand. She had much to learn in the matter of cooking over a camp-fire, and made fair progress, discovering, first of all, that control of the fire meant far more than the size of it. When the coffee was boiled, she settled the grounds with a part-cup of cold water and placed the pot on the edge of the coals where it would keep hot and yet not boil. She fried potato dollars and onions in the same pan, but separately, and set them on top of the coffee pot in the tin plate she was to eat from, covering it with Billy's inverted plate. On the dry hot pan, in the way that delighted Billy, she fried the steak. This completed, and while Billy poured the coffee, she served the steak, putting the dollars and onions back into the frying pan for a moment to make them piping hot again.

"What more d'ye want than this?" Billy challenged with deep-toned satisfaction, in the pause after his final cup of coffee, while he rolled a cigarette. He lay on his side, full length, resting on his

31

elbow. The fire was burning brightly, and Saxon's color was heightened by the flickering flames. "Now our folks, when they was on the move, had to be afraid for Indians, and wild animals and all sorts of things; an' here we are, as safe as bugs in a rug. Take this sand. What better bed could you ask? Soft as feathers. Say—you look good to me, heap little squaw. I bet you don't look an inch over sixteen right now, Mrs. Babe-in-the-Woods."

"Don't I?" she glowed, with a flirt of the head sideward and a white flash of teeth. "If you weren't smoking a cigarette I'd ask you if your mother knew you're out, Mr. Babe-in-the-Sandbank."

"Say," he began, with transparently feigned seriousness. "I want to ask you something, if you don't mind. Now, of course, I don't want to hurt your feelin's or nothin', but just the same there's something important I'd like to know."

"Well, what is it?" she inquired, after a fruitless wait.

"Well, it's just this, Saxon. I like you like anything an' all that, but here's night come on, an' we're a thousand miles from anywhere, and—well, what I wanta know is: are we really an' truly married, you an' me?"

"Really and truly," she assured him. "Why?"

"Oh, nothing; but I'd kind a-forgotten, an' I was gettin' embarrassed, you know, because if we wasn't, seein' the way I was brought up, this'd be no place—"

"That will do you," she said severely. "And this is just the time and place for you to get in the firewood for morning while I wash up the dishes and put the kitchen in order."

He started to obey but paused to throw his arm about her and draw her close. Neither spoke, but when he went his way Saxon's breast was fluttering and a song of thanksgiving breathed on her lips.

The night had come on, dim with the light of faint stars. But these had disappeared behind clouds that seemed to have arisen from nowhere. It was the beginning of California Indian summer. The air was warm, with just the first hint of evening chill, and there was no wind.

"I've a feeling as if we've just started to live," Saxon said, when Billy, his firewood collected, joined her on the blankets before the fire. "I've learned more to-day than ten years in Oakland." She drew a long breath and braced her shoulders. "Farming's a bigger subject than I thought."

Billy said nothing. With steady eyes he was staring into the fire, and she knew he was turning something over in his mind.

"What is it?" she asked, when she saw he had reached a conclusion, at the same time resting her hand on the back of his.

"Just ben framin' up that ranch of ourn," he answered. "It's all well enough, these dinky farmlets. They'll do for foreigners. But we Americans just gotta have room. I want to be able to look at a hill-top an' know it's my land, and know it's my land down the other side an' up the next hilltop, an' know that over beyond that, down alongside some creek, my mares are most likely grazin', an' their little colts grazin' with 'em or kickin' up their heels. You know, there's money in raisin' horses—especially the big workhorses that run to eighteen hundred an' two thousand pounds. They're payin' for 'em, in the cities, every day in the year, seven an' eight hundred a pair, matched geldings, four years old. Good pasture an' plenty of it, in this kind of a climate, is all they need, along with some sort of shelter an' a little hay in long spells of bad weather. I never thought of it before, but let me tell you that this ranch proposition is begin-nin' to look good to me."

Saxon was all excitement. Here was new information on the cher-ished subject, and, best of all, Billy was the authority. Still better, he was taking an interest himself.

"There'll be room for that and for everything on a quarter sec-tion," she encouraged.

"Sure thing. Around the house we'll have vegetables an' fruit and chickens an' everything, just like the Porchugeeze, an' plenty of room beside to walk around an' range the horses."

"But won't the colts cost money, Billy?"

"Not much. The cobblestones eat horses up fast. That's where I'll get my brood mares, from the ones knocked out by the city. I know that end of it. They sell 'em at auction, an' they're good for years an' years, only no good on the cobbles any more."

There ensued a long pause. In the dying fire both were busy vi-sioning the farm to be.

"It's pretty still, ain't it?" Billy said, rousing himself at last. He gazed about him. "An' black as a stack of black cats." He shivered, buttoned his coat, and tossed several sticks on the fire. "Just the same, it's the best kind of a climate in the world. Many's the time, when I was a little kid, I've heard my father brag about California's bein' a blanket climate. He went East, once, an' staid a summer an' a winter, an' got all he wanted. Never again for him."

"My mother said there never was such a land for climate. How wonderful it must have seemed to them after crossing the deserts and mountains. They called it the land of milk and honey. The ground was so rich that all they needed to do was scratch it, Cady used to say."

"And wild game everywhere," Billy contributed. "Mr. Roberts, the one that adopted my father, he drove cattle from the San Joaquin to the Columbia river. He had forty men helpin' him, an' all they took along was powder an' salt. They lived off the game they shot."

"The hills were full of deer, and my mother saw whole herds of elk around Santa Rosa. Some time we'll go there, Billy. I've always wanted to."

"And when my father was a young man, somewhere up north of Sacramento, in a creek called Cache Slough, the tules was full of grizzlies. He used to go in an' shoot 'em. An' when they caught 'em in the open, he an' the Mexicans used to ride up an' rope them—catch them with lariats, you know. He said a horse that wasn't afraid of grizzlies fetched ten times as much as any other horse. An' panthers!—all the old folks called 'em painters an' catamounts an' varmints. Yes, we'll go to Santa Rosa some time. Maybe we won't like that land down the coast, an' have to keep on hikin'."

By this time the fire had died down, and Saxon had finished brushing and braiding her hair. Their bed-going preliminaries were simple, and in a few minutes they were side by side under the blankets. . . .

At the first gray of dawn, Billy crawled out and built a roaring fire. Saxon drew up to it shiveringly. They were hollow-eyed and weary. Saxon began to laugh. Billy joined sulkily, then brightened up as his eyes chanced upon the coffee pot, which he immediately put on to boil.

It is forty miles from Oakland to San José, and Saxon and Billy accomplished it in three easy days. No more obliging and angrily garrulous linemen were encountered, and few were the opportunities for conversation with chance wayfarers. Numbers of tramps, carrying rolls of blankets, were met, traveling both north and south on the county road; and from talks with them Saxon quickly learned that they knew little or nothing about farming. They were mostly old men, feeble or besotted, and all they knew was work—where jobs might be good, where jobs had been good; but the places they mentioned were always a long way off. . . .

Early in the afternoon, on the outskirts of San José, Saxon called a halt.

"I'm going right in there and talk," she declared, "unless they set the dogs on me. That's the prettiest place yet, isn't it?"

Billy, who was always visioning hills and spacious ranges for his horses, mumbled unenthusiastic assent.

"And the vegetables! Look at them! And the flowers growing along the borders! That beats tomato plants in wrapping paper."

"Don't see the sense of it," Billy objected. "Where's the money come in from flowers that take up the ground that good vegetables might be growin' on?"

"And that's what I'm going to find out." She pointed to a woman, stooped to the ground and working with a trowel, in front of the tiny bungalow. "I don't know what she's like, but at the worst she can only be mean. See! She's looking at us now. Drop your load alongside of mine, and come on in."

. . . The woman stood up and turned from her flowers, and Saxon saw that she was middle-aged, slender, and simply but nicely dressed. She wore glasses, and Saxon's reading of her face was that it was kind but nervous looking.

"I don't want anything to-day," she said, before Saxon could speak, administering the rebuff with a pleasant smile.

Saxon groaned inwardly over the black-covered telescope basket. Evidently the woman had seen her put it down.

"We're not peddling," she explained quickly.

"Oh, I am sorry for the mistake."

This time the women's smile was even pleasanter, and she waited for Saxon to state her errand.

Nothing loath, Saxon took it at a plunge.

"We're looking for land. We want to be farmers, you know, and before we get the land we want to find out what kind of land we want. And seeing your pretty place has just filled me up with questions. You see, we don't know anything about farming. We've lived in the city all our life, and now we've given it up and are going to live in the country and be happy."

She paused. The woman's face seemed to grow quizzical, though the pleasantness did not abate.

"But how do you know you will be happy in the country?" she asked.

"I don't know. All I do know is that poor people can't be happy in the city where they have labor troubles all the time. If they can't be happy in the country, then there's no happiness anywhere, and that doesn't seem fair, does it?"

"It is sound reasoning, my dear, as far as it goes. But you must remember that there are many poor people in the country and many unhappy people."

"You look neither poor nor unhappy," Saxon challenged.

"You *are* a dear."

Saxon saw the pleased flush in the other's face, which lingered as she went on.

"But still. I may be peculiarly qualified to live and succeed in the country. As you saw yourself, you've spent your life in the city. You don't know the first thing about the country. It might even break your heart."

Saxon's mind went back to the terrible months in the Pine Street cottage.

"I know already that the city will break my heart. Maybe the country will, too, but just the same it's my only chance, don't you see. It's that or nothing. Besides, our folks before us were all of the country. It seems the more natural way. And better, here I am, which proves that 'way down inside I must want the country, must, as you call it, be peculiarly qualified for the country, or else I wouldn't be here."

The other nodded approval, and looked at her with growing interest.

"That young man—" she began.

"Is my husband. He was a teamster until the big strike came. My name is Roberts, Saxon Roberts, and my husband is William Roberts."

"And I am Mrs. Mortimer," the other said, with a bow of acknowledgment. "I am a widow. And now, if you will ask your husband in, I shall try to answer some of your many questions. Tell him to put the bundles inside the gate. . . . And now what are all the questions you are filled with?"

"Oh, all kinds. How does it pay? How did you manage it all? How much did the land cost? Did you build that beautiful house? How much do you pay the men? How did you learn all the different kinds of things, and which grew best and which paid best? What is the best way to sell them? How do you sell them?" Saxon paused and laughed. "Oh, I haven't begun yet. Why do you have flowers on the borders everywhere? I looked over the Portuguese farms around San Leandro, but they never mixed flowers and vegetables."

Mrs. Mortimer held up her land. "Let me answer the last first. It is the key to almost everything."

But Billy arrived, and the explanation was deferred until after his introduction.

"The flowers caught your eyes, didn't they, my dear?" Mrs. Mortimer resumed. "And brought you in through my gate and right up to me. And that's the very reason they were planted with the vegetables—to catch eyes. You can't imagine how many eyes they have caught, nor how many owners of eyes they have lured inside my gate. This is a good road, and is a very popular short country drive for townsfolk. Oh, no; I've never had any luck with automobiles.

They can't see anything for dust. But I began when nearly everybody still used carriages. The townswomen would drive by. My flowers, and then my place, would catch their eyes. They would tell their drivers to stop. And—well, somehow, I managed to be in the front within speaking distance. Usually I succeeded in inviting them in to see my flowers . . . and vegetables, of course. Everything was sweet, clean, pretty. It all appealed. And—" Mrs. Mortimer shrugged her shoulders. "It is well known that the stomach sees through the eyes. The thought of vegetables growing among flowers pleased their fancy. They wanted my vegetables. They must have them. And they did, at double the market price, which they were only too glad to pay. You see, I became the fashion, or a fad, in a small way. Nobody lost. The vegetables were certainly good, as good as any on the market and often fresher. And, besides, my customers killed two birds with one stone; for they were pleased with themselves for philanthropic reasons. Not only did they obtain the finest and freshest possible vegetables, but at the same time they were happy with the knowledge that they were helping a deserving widow-woman. Yes, and it gave a certain tone to their establishments to be able to say they bought Mrs. Mortimer's vegetables. But that's too big a side to go into. In short, my little place became a show place—anywhere to go, for a drive or anything, you know, when time has to be killed. And it became noised about who I was, and who my husband had been, what I had been. Some of the townsladies I had known personally in the old days. They actually worked for my success. And then, too, I used to serve tea. My patrons became my guests for the time being. I still serve it, when they drive out to show me off to their friends. So you see, the flowers are one of the ways I succeeded."

Saxon was glowing with appreciation, but Mrs. Mortimer, glancing at Billy, noted not entire approval. His blue eyes were clouded.

"Well, out with it," she encouraged. "What are you thinking?"

To Saxon's surprise, he answered directly, and to her double surprise, his criticism was of a nature which had never entered her head.

"It's just a trick," Billy expounded. "That's what I was gettin' at—"

"But a paying trick," Mrs. Mortimer interrupted, her eyes dancing and vivacious behind the glasses.

"Yes, and no," Billy said stubbornly, speaking in his slow, deliberate fashion. "If every farmer was to mix flowers an' vegetables, then every farmer would get double the market price, an' then there wouldn't be any double market price. Everything'd be as it was before."

"You are opposing a theory to a fact," Mrs. Mortimer stated. "The fact is that all the farmers do not do it. The fact is that I do receive double the price. You can't get away from that."

Billy was unconvinced, though unable to reply.

"Just the same," he muttered, with a slow shake of the head, "I don't get the hang of it. There's something wrong so far as we're concerned—my wife an' me, I mean. Maybe I'll get hold of it after a while."

"And in the meantime, we'll look around," Mrs. Mortimer invited. "I want to show you everything, and tell you how I make it go. Afterward, we'll sit down, and I'll tell you about the beginning. You see—" she bent her gaze on Saxon—"I want you thoroughly to understand that you can succeed in the country if you go about it right. I didn't know a thing about it when I began, and I didn't have a fine big man like yours. I was all alone. But I'll tell you about that."

For the next hour, among vegetables, berry-bushes and fruit trees, Saxon stored her brain with a huge mass of information to be digested at her leisure. Billy, too, was interested, but he left the talking to Saxon, himself rarely asking a question. At the rear of the bungalow, where everything was as clean and orderly as the front, they were shown through the chicken yard. Here, in different runs, were kept several hundred small and snow-white hens.

"White Leghorns," said Mrs. Mortimer. "You have no idea what they netted me this year. I never keep a hen a moment past the prime of her laying period—"

"Just what I was tellin' you, Saxon, about horses," Billy broke in.

"And by the simplest method of hatching them at the right time, which not one farmer in ten thousand ever dreams of doing, I have them laying in the winter when most hens stop laying and when eggs are highest. Another thing: I have my special customers. They pay me ten cents a dozen more than the market price, because my specialty is one-day eggs."

Here she chanced to glance at Billy, and guessed that he was still wrestling with his problem.

"Same old thing?" she queried.

He nodded. "Same old thing. If every farmer delivered day-old eggs, there wouldn't be no ten cents higher'n the top price. They'd be no better off then they was before."

"But the eggs would be one-day eggs, all the eggs would be one-day eggs, you mustn't forget that," Mrs. Mortimer pointed out.

"But that don't butter no toast for my wife an' me," he objected. "An' that's what I've ben tryin' to get the hang of, an' now I got it.

You talk about theory an' fact. Ten cents higher than top price is a theory to Saxon an' me. The fact is, we ain't got no eggs, no chickens, an' no land for the chickens to run an' lay eggs on."

Their hostess nodded sympathetically.

"An' there's something else about this outfit of yourn that I don't get the hang of," he pursued. "I can't just put my finger on it, but it's there all right."

They were shown over the cattery, the piggery, the milkery, and the kennelry, as Mrs. Mortimer called her livestock departments. None was large. All were money-makers, she assured them, and rattled off her profits glibly. She took their breaths away by the prices given and received for pedigreed Persians, pedigreed Ohio Improved Chester, pedigreed Scotch collies, and pedigreed Jerseys. For the milk of the last she also had a special private market, receiving five cents more a quart than was fetched by the best dairy milk. Billy was quick to point out the difference between the look of her orchard and the look of the orchard they had inspected the previous afternoon, and Mrs. Mortimer showed him scores of other differences, many of which he was compelled to accept on faith.

Then she told them of another industry, her home-made jams and jellies, always contracted for in advance, and at prices dizzyingly beyond the regular market. They sat in comfortable rattan chairs on the veranda, while she told the story of how she had drummed up the jam and jelly trade, dealing only with the one best restaurant and one best club in San José. To the proprietor and the steward she had gone with her samples, in long discussions beaten down their opposition, overcome their reluctance, and persuaded tho pro prietor, in particular, to make a "special" of her wares, to boom them quietly with his patrons, and, above all, to charge stiffly for dishes and courses in which they appeared.

Throughout the recital Billy's eyes were moody with dissatisfaction. Mrs. Mortimer saw, and waited.

"And now, begin at the beginning," Saxon begged.

But Mrs. Mortimer refused unless they agreed to stop for supper. Saxon frowned Billy's reluctance away, and accepted for both of them.

"Well, then," Mrs. Mortimer took up her tale, "in the beginning I was a greenhorn, city born and bred. All I knew of the country was that it was a place to go to for vacations, and I always went to springs and mountain and seaside resorts. I had lived among books almost all my life. I was head librarian of the Doncaster Library for years. Then I married Mr. Mortimer. He was a book man, a professor in San Miguel University. He had a long sickness, and when he died there was nothing left. Even his life insurance was eaten into before I could be free of creditors. As for myself, I was worn out, on the verge of nervous prostration, fit for nothing. I had five thousand dollars left, however, and, without going into the details, I decided to go farming. I found this place, in a delightful climate, close to San José—the end of the electric line is only a quarter of a mile on— and I bought it. I paid two thousand cash, and gave a mortgage for two thousand. It cost two hundred an acre, you see."

"Twenty acres!" Saxon cried.

"Wasn't that pretty small?" Billy ventured.

"Too large, oceans too large. I leased ten acres of it the first thing. And it's still leased after all this time. Even the ten I'd retained was much too large for a long, long time. It's only now that I'm beginning to feel a tiny mite crowded."

"And ten acres has supported you an' two hired men?" Billy demanded, amazed.

Mrs. Mortimer clapped her hands delightedly.

"Listen. I had been a librarian. I knew my way among books. First of all I'd read everything written on the subject, and subscribed to some of the best farm magazines and papers. And you ask if my ten acres have supported me and two hired men. Let me tell you. I have four hired men. The ten acres certainly must support them, as it supports Hannah—she's a Swedish widow who runs the house and who is a perfect Trojan during the jam and jelly season—and Hannah's daughter, who goes to school and lends a hand, and my nephew whom I have taken to raise and educate. Also, the ten acres have come pretty close to paying for the whole twenty, as well as for this house, and all the outbuildings, and all the pedigreed stock."

Saxon remembered what the young lineman had said about the Portuguese.

"The ten acres didn't do a bit of it," she cried. "It was your head that did it all, and you know it."

"And that's the point, my dear. It shows the right kind of person can succeed in the country. Remember, the soil is generous. But it must be treated generously, and that is something the old style American farmer can't get into his head. . . .

"I'm of the old stock myself." Mrs. Mortimer went on proudly. "My grandmother was one of the survivors of the Donner Party. My grandfather, Jason Whitney, came around the Horn and took part in the raising of the Bear Flag at Sonoma. He was at Monterey when John Marshall discovered gold in Sutter's mill-race. One of the streets in San Francisco is named after him."

"I know it," Billy put in. "Whitney Street. It's near Russian Hill. Saxon's mother walked across the Plains."

"And Billy's grandfather and grandmother were massacred by the Indians," Saxon contributed. "His father was a little baby boy, and lived with the Indians, until captured by the whites. He didn't even know his name and was adopted by a Mr. Roberts."

"Why, you two dear children, we're almost like relatives." Mrs. Mortimer beamed. "It's a breath of old times, alas! all forgotten in these fly-away days. I am especially interested, because I've catalogued and read everything covering those times. You—" she indicated Billy, "you are historical, or at least your father is. I remember about him. The whole thing is in Bancroft's History. It was the Modoc Indians. There were eighteen wagons. Your father was the only survivor, a mere baby at the time, with no knowledge of what happened. He was adopted by the leader of the whites."

"That's right," said Billy. "It was the Modocs. His train must have ben bound for Oregon. It was all wiped out. I wonder if you know anything about Saxon's mother. She used to write poetry in the early days."

"Was any of it printed?"

"Yes," Saxon answered. "In the old San José papers."

"And do you know any of it?"

"Yes, there's one beginning:

"   'Sweet as the wind-lute's airy strains
       Your gentle muse has learned to sing,
   And California's boundless plains
       Prolong the soft notes echoing.' "

"It sounds familiar," Mrs. Mortimer said, pondering. ". . . I don't remember your mother's name."

"It was Daisy—" Saxon began.

"No; Dayelle," Mrs. Mortimer corrected with quickening recollection.

"Oh, but nobody called her that."

"But she signed it that way. What is the rest?"

"Daisy Wiley Brown."

Mrs. Mortimer went to the bookshelves and quickly returned with a large, soberly-bound volume.

. . . Mrs. Mortimer's glasses required repolishing; and for half an hour she and Billy remained silent while Saxon devoured her mother's lines. At the end, staring at the book which she had closed on her finger, she could only repeat in wondering awe:

"And I never knew, I never knew."

But during that half hour Mrs. Mortimer's mind had not been idle. A little later, she broached her plan. She believed in intensive dairying as well as intensive farming, and intended, as soon as the lease expired, to establish a Jersey dairy on the other ten acres. This, like everything she had done, would be model, and it meant that she would require more help. Billy and Saxon were just the two. By next summer she could have them installed in the cottage she intended building. In the meantime she could arrange, one way and another, to get work for Billy through the winter. She would guarantee this work, and she knew a small house they could rent just at the end of the car-line. Under her supervision Billy could take charge from the very beginning of the building. In this way they would be earning money, preparing themselves for independent farming life, and have opportunity to look about them.

But her persuasions were vain. In the end Saxon succinctly epitomized their point of view.

"We can't stop at the first place, even if it is as beautiful and kind as yours and as nice as this valley is. We don't even know what we want. We've got to go farther, and see all kinds of places and all kinds of ways, in order to find out. We're not in a hurry to make up our minds. We want to make, oh, so very sure! And besides . . ." She hesitated. "Besides, we don't like altogether flat land. Billy wants some hills in his. And so do I."

When they were ready to leave Mrs. Mortimer offered to present Saxon with "The Story of the Files"; but Saxon shook her head and got some money from Billy.

"It says it costs two dollars," she said. "Will you buy me one, and keep it till we get settled? Then I'll write, and you can send it to me."

"Oh, you Americans," Mrs. Mortimer chided, accepting the money. "But you must promise to write from time to time before you're settled."

She saw them to the county road.

"You are brave young things," she said at parting. "I only wish I were going with you, my pack upon my back. You're perfectly glorious, the pair of you. If ever I can do anything for you, just let me know. You're bound to succeed, and I want a hand in it myself. Let me know how that government land turns out, though I warn you I haven't much faith in its feasibility. It's sure to be too far away from markets."

She shook hands with Billy. Saxon she caught into her arms and kissed.

"Be brave," she said, with low earnestness, in Saxon's ear. "You'll win. You are starting with the right ideas. And you were right not to accept my proposition. But remember, it, or better, will always be open to you. You're young yet, both of you. Don't be in a hurry. Any time you stop anywhere for a while, let me know, and I'll mail you heaps of agricultural reports and farm publications. Good-bye. Heaps and heaps and heaps of luck."

THEY had taken the direct county road across the hills from Monterey, instead of the Seventeen Mile Drive around by the coast, so that Carmel Bay came upon them without any fore-glimmerings of its beauty. Dropping down through the pungent pines, they passed woods-embowered cottages, quaint and rustic, of artists and writers, and went on across wind-blown rolling sandhills held to place by sturdy lupins and nodding with pale California poppies. Saxon screamed in sudden wonder of delight, then caught her breath and gazed at the amazing peacock-blue of a breaker, shot through with golden sunlight, overfalling in a mile-long sweep and thundering into white ruin of foam on a crescent beach of sand scarcely less white.

How long they stood and watched the stately procession of breakers, rising from out the deep and wind-capped sea to froth and thunder at their feet, Saxon did not know. She was recalled to herself when Billy, laughing, tried to remove the telescope basket from her shoulders.

"You kind of look as though you was goin' to stop a while," he said. "So we might as well get comfortable."

"I never dreamed it, I never dreamed it," she repeated, with passionately clasped hands. "I . . . I thought the surf at the Cliff House was wonderful, but it gave no idea of this. —Oh! Look! LOOK! Did you ever see such an unspeakable color? And the sunlight flashing right through it! Oh! Oh! Oh!"

At last she was able to take her eyes from the surf and gaze at the sea-horizon of deepest peacock-blue and piled with cloud-masses, at the curve of the beach south to the jagged point of rocks, and at the rugged blue mountains seen across soft low hills, landward, up Carmel Valley.

"Might as well sit down an' take it easy," Billy indulged her. "This is too good to want to run away from all at once."

Saxon assented, but began immediately to unlace her shoes.

"You ain't a-goin' to?" Billy asked in surprised delight, then began unlacing his own.

But before they were ready to run barefooted on the perilous fringe of cream-wet sand where land and ocean met, a new and wonderful thing attracted their attention. Down from the dark pines and across the sandhills ran a man, naked save for narrow trunks. He was smooth and rosy-skinned, cherubic-faced, with a thatch of curly yellow hair, but his body was hugely thewed as a Hercules'.

"Gee!—must be Sandow," Billy muttered low to Saxon.

But she was thinking of the engraving in her mother's scrapbook and of the Vikings on the wet sands of England.

The runner passed them a dozen feet away, crossed the wet sand, never pausing, till the froth wash was to his knees while above him, ten feet at least, upreared a wall of overtopping water. Huge and powerful as his body had seemed, it was now white and fragile in the face of that imminent, great-handed buffet of the sea. Saxon gasped with anxiety, and she stole a look at Billy to note that he was tense with watching.

But the stranger sprang to meet the blow, and just when it seemed he must be crushed, he dived into the face of the breaker and disappeared. The mighty mass of water fell in thunder on the beach, but beyond appeared a yellow head, one arm out-reaching, and a portion of a shoulder. Only a few strokes was he able to make ere he was compelled to dive through another breaker. This was the battle—to win seaward against the sweep of the shoreward-hastening sea. Each time he dived and lost to view Saxon caught her breath and clenched her hands. Sometimes, after the passage of a breaker, they could not find him, and when they did he would be scores of feet away, flung there like a chip by a smoke-bearded breaker. Often it seemed he must fail and be thrown upon the beach, but at the end of half an hour he was beyond the outer edge of the surf and swimming strong, no longer diving, but topping the waves. Soon he was so far away that only at intervals could they find the speck of him. That, too, vanished, and Saxon and Billy looked at each other, she with amazement at the swimmer's valor, Billy with blue eyes flashing.

"Some swimmer, that boy, some swimmer," he praised. "Nothing chicken-hearted about him. —Say, I only know tank-swimmin', an' bay-swimmin', but now I'm goin' to learn ocean-swimmin'. If I could do that I'd be so proud you couldn't come within forty feet of me. Why, Saxon, honest to God, I'd sooner do what he done than own a thousan' farms. Oh, I can swim, too, I'm tellin' you, like a fish—I swum, one Sunday, from the Narrow Gauge Pier to Sessions' Basin, an' that's miles—but I never seen anything like that guy in the swimmin' line. An' I'm not goin' to leave this beach until he comes back. —All by his lonely out there in a mountain sea, think of it! He's got his nerve all right, all right."

Saxon and Billy ran barefooted up and down the beach, pursuing each other with brandished snakes of seaweed and playing like children for an hour. It was not until they were putting on their shoes that they sighted the yellow head bearing shoreward. Billy was at the edge of the surf to meet him, emerging, not white-skinned as he had entered, but red from the pounding he had received at the hands of the sea.

"You're a wonder, and I just got to hand it to you," Billy greeted him in outspoken admiration.

"It *was* a big surf to-day," the young man replied, with a nod of acknowledgment.

"It don't happen that you are a fighter I never heard of?" Billy queried, striving to get some inkling of the identity of the physical prodigy.

The other laughed and shook his head, and Billy could not guess that he was an ex-captain of a 'Varsity Eleven, and incidentally the father of a family and the author of many books. He looked Billy over with an eye trained in measuring freshmen aspirants for the gridiron.

"You're some body of a man," he appreciated. "You'd strip with the best of them. Am I right in guessing that you know your way about in the ring?"

Billy nodded. "My name's Roberts."

The swimmer scowled with a futile effort at recollection.

"Bill—Bill Roberts," Billy supplemented.

"Oh, ho!—Not *Big* Bill Roberts? Why, I saw you fight, before the earthquake, in the Mechanic's Pavilion. It was a preliminary to Eddie Hanlon and some other fellow. You're a two-handed fighter, I remember that, with an awful wallop, but slow. Yes, I remember, you were slow that night, but you got your man." He put out a wet hand. "My name's Hazard—Jim Hazard."

"An' if you're the football coach that was, a couple of years ago, I've read about you in the papers. Am I right?"

They shook hands heartily, and Saxon was introduced. She felt very small beside the two young giants, and very proud, withal, that she belonged to the race that gave them birth. She could only listen to them talk.

"I'd like to put on the gloves with you every day for half an hour," Hazard said. "You could teach me a lot. Are you going to stay around here?"

"No. We're goin' on down the coast, lookin' for land. Just the same, I could teach you a few, and there's one thing you could teach me—surf-swimmin'."

"I'll swap lessons with you any time," Hazard offered. He turned to Saxon. "Why don't you stop in Carmel for a while? It isn't so bad."

"It's beautiful," she acknowledged, with a grateful smile, "but—" She turned and pointed to their packs on the edge of the lupins. "We're on the tramp, and lookin' for government land."

"If you're looking down past the Sur for it, it will keep," he laughed. "Well, I've got to run along and get some clothes on. If you come back this way, look me up. Anybody will tell you where I live. So long."

And, as he had first arrived, he departed, crossing the sandhills on the run.

Billy followed him with admiring eyes.

"Some boy, some boy," he murmured. "Why, Saxon, he's famous. If I've seen his face in the papers once, I've seen it a thousand times. An' he ain't a bit stuck on himself. Just man to man. Say! —I'm beginnin' to have faith in the old stock again."

They turned their backs on the beach and in the tiny main street bought meat, vegetables, and half a dozen eggs. Billy had to drag Saxon away from the window of a fascinating shop where were iridescent pearls of abalone, set and unset.

"Abalones grow here, all along the coast," Billy assured her; "an' I'll get you all you want. Low tide's the time."

"My father had a set of cuff-buttons made of abalone shell," she said. "They were set in pure, soft gold. I haven't thought about them for years, and I wonder who has them now."

They turned south. Everywhere from among the pines peeped the quaint pretty houses of the artist folk, and they were not prepared, where the road dipped to Carmel River, for the building that met their eyes.

"I know what it is," Saxon almost whispered. "It's an old Spanish Mission. It's the Carmel Mission, of course. That's the way the Spaniards came up from Mexico, building missions as they came and converting the Indians—"

"Until we chased them out, Spaniards an' Indians, whole kit an' caboodle," Billy observed with calm satisfaction.

"Just the same, it's wonderful," Saxon mused, gazing at the big, half-ruined adobe structure. "There is the Mission Dolores, in San Francisco, but it's smaller than this and not as old."

Hidden from the sea by low hillocks, forsaken by human being and human habitation, the church of sun-baked clay and straw and chalk-rock stood hushed and breathless in the midst of the adobe ruins which once had housed its worshiping thousands. The spirit

46

of the place descended upon Saxon and Billy, and they walked softly, speaking in whispers, almost afraid to go in through the open portal. There was neither priest nor worshiper, yet they found all the evidences of use, by a congregation which Billy judged must be small from the number of the benches. Later they climbed the earthquake-cracked belfry, noting the hand-hewn timbers; and in the gallery, discovering the pure quality of their voices, Saxon, trembling at her own temerity, softly sang the opening bars of "Jesus Lover of My Soul." Delighted with the result, she leaned over the railing, gradually increasing her voice to its full strength as she sang. . . .

Billy leaned against the ancient wall and loved her with his eyes, and, when she had finished, he murmured, almost in a whisper:

"That was beautiful—just beautiful. An' you ought to a-seen your face when you sang. It was as beautiful as your voice. Ain't it funny—I never think of religion except when I think of you."

They camped in the willow bottom, cooked dinner, and spent the afternoon on the point of low rocks north of the mouth of the river. They had not intended to spend the afternoon, but found themselves too fascinated to turn away from the breakers bursting upon the rocks and from the many kinds of colorful sea life—starfish, crabs, mussels, sea anemones, and, once, in a rock-pool, a small devilfish that chilled their blood when it cast the hooded net of its body around the small crabs they tossed to it. As the tide grew lower, they gathered a mess of mussels—huge fellows, five and six inches long and bearded like patriarchs. Then, while Billy wandered in a vain search for abalones, Saxon lay and dabbled in the crystal-clear water of a rock-pool, dipping up handfuls of glistening jewels—ground bits of shell and pebble of flashing rose and blue and green and violet. Billy came back and lay beside her, lazying in the sea-cool sunshine, and together they watched the sun sink into the horizon where the ocean was deepest peacock-blue.

She reached out her hand to Billy's and sighed with sheer repletion of content. It seemed she had never lived such a wonderful day. It was as if all old dreams were coming true. Such beauty of the world she had never guessed in her fondest imagining. Billy pressed her hand tenderly.

"What was you thinkin' of?" he asked, as they arose finally to go.

"Oh, I don't know, Billy. Perhaps that it was better, one day like this, than ten thousand years in Oakland."

4.

On Sonoma Mountain

SELECTIONS FROM BURNING DAYLIGHT

This novel of adventure in the Klondike, high finance in New York and the West, and spiritual regeneration in California's Sonoma County made its debut as a serialization in The New York Herald from June 19, 1909, to April 28, 1910. The Macmillan Company, London's most consistent book publisher, brought out the first edition in October 1910.

Elam Harnish (alias "Burning Daylight"), the hero of this story, makes a fortune in the gold fields and then increases his wealth in California through shrewd financial investments. But his quest for more money gradually destroys his integrity and physical well-being. Dede Mason, the young woman he hopes to marry, makes him painfully aware of what he has become. "You are not the same man at all, and your money is destroying you," she exclaims. "You are becoming something not so healthy, not so clean, not so nice."

In the selections here (from chapters VIII and IX), Daylight begins his self-renewal when he spends a weekend in Sonoma County. On a leisurely horseback ride along the ravines and up to the summit of Sonoma Mountain, he becomes aware of the simple beauties of nature and the countryside—a part of the world he had virtually forgotten about—which starts him on a path to his own salvation.

The first barn built on London's Beauty Ranch. This countryside figures promi-
nently in *The Valley of the Moon* and *Burning Daylight*.

ON SONOMA MOUNTAIN

DAYLIGHT'S COMING TO CIVILIZATION HAD NOT IMPROVED him. True, he wore better clothes, had learned slightly better manners, and spoke better English. As a gambler and a man-trampler he had developed remarkable efficiency. Also, he had become used to a higher standard of living, and he had whetted his wits to razor sharpness in the fierce, complicated struggle of fighting males. But he had hardened, and at the expense of his old-time, whole-souled geniality. Of the essential refinements of civilization he knew nothing. He did not know they existed. He had become cynical, bitter, and brutal. Power had its effect on him that it had on all men. Suspicious of the big exploiters, despising the fools of the exploited herd, he had faith only in himself. This led to an undue and erroneous exaltation of his ego, while kindly consideration of others—nay, even simple respect—was destroyed, until naught was left for him but to worship at the shrine of self.

Physically, he was not the man of iron muscles who had come down out of the Arctic. He did not exercise sufficiently, ate more than was good for him, and drank altogether too much. His muscles were getting flabby, and his tailor called attention to his increasing waistband. In fact, Daylight was developing a definite paunch. This physical deterioration was manifest likewise in his face. The lean Indian visage was suffering a city change. The slight hollows in the cheeks under the high cheek-bones had filled out. The beginning of puff-sacks under the eyes was faintly visible. The girth of the neck had increased; and the first crease and fold of a double chin were becoming plainly discernible. The old effect of asceticism, bred of terrific hardships and toil, had vanished; the features had become broader and heavier, betraying all the stigmata of the life he lived, advertising the man's self-indulgence, harshness, and brutality.

Even his human affiliations were descending. Playing a lone hand, contemptuous of most of the men with whom he played, lacking in sympathy or understanding of them, and certainly independent of them, he found little in common with those to be encountered, say at the Alta-Pacific. In point of fact, when the battle with the steamship companies was at its height and his raid was inflicting incalculable damage on all business interests, he had been asked to resign from the Alta-Pacific. The idea had been rather to his liking, and he had found new quarters in clubs like the Riverside, organized and practically maintained by the city bosses. He found that he really liked such men better. They were more primitive and simple, and they did not put on airs. They were honest buccaneers, frankly in the game for what they could get out of it, on the surface more raw and savage, but at least not glossed over with oily or graceful hypocrisy. The Alta-Pacific had suggested that his resignation be kept a private matter, and then had privily informed the newspapers. The latter had made great capital out of the forced resignation, but Daylight had grinned and silently gone his way, though registering a black mark against more than one club member who was destined to feel, in the days to come, the crushing weight of the Klondiker's financial paw.

The storm-centre of a combined newspaper attack lasting for months, Daylight's character had been torn to shreds. There was no fact in his history that had not been distorted into a criminality or a vice. This public making of him over into an iniquitous monster had pretty well crushed any lingering hope he had of getting acquainted with Dede Mason. He felt that there was no chance for her ever to look kindly on a man of his caliber, and, beyond increasing her salary to seventy-five dollars a month, he proceeded gradually to forget about her. The increase was made known to her through Morrison, and later she thanked Daylight, and that was the end of it.

One week-end, feeling heavy and depressed and tired of the city and its ways, he obeyed the impulse of a whim that was later to play an important part in his life. The desire to get out of the city for a whiff of country air and for a change of scene was the cause. Yet, to himself, he made the excuse of going to Glen Ellen for the purpose of inspecting the brickyard with which Holdsworthy had goldbricked him.

He spent the night in the little country hotel, and on Sunday morning, astride a saddle-horse rented from the Glen Ellen butcher, rode out of the village. The brickyard was close at hand on the flat beside the Sonoma Creek. The kilns were visible among the trees, when he glanced to the left and caught sight of a cluster of wooded knolls half a mile away, perched on the rolling slopes of Sonoma Mountain. The mountain, itself wooded, towered behind. The trees on the knolls seemed to beckon to him. The dry, early-summer air, shot through with sunshine, was wine to him. Unconsciously he drank it in in deep breaths. The prospect of the brickyard was uninviting. He was jaded with all things business, and the wooded knolls were calling to him. A horse was between his legs—a good horse, he decided; one that sent him back to the cayuses he had ridden during his eastern Oregon boyhood. He had been somewhat of a rider in those early days, and the champ of bit and crack of saddle-leather sounded good to him now.

Resolving to have his fun first, and to look over the brickyard afterward, he rode on up the hill, prospecting for a way across country to get to the knolls. He left the country road at the first gate he came to and cantered through a hayfield. The grain was waist-high on either side the wagon road, and he sniffed the warm aroma of it with delighted nostrils. Larks flew up before him, and from everywhere came mellow notes. From the appearance of the road it was patent that it had been used for hauling clay to the now idle brickyard. Salving his conscience with the idea that this was part of the inspection, he rode on to the clay-pit—a huge scar in a hillside. But he did not linger long, swinging off again to the left and leaving the road. Not a farm-house was in sight, and the change from the city crowding was essentially satisfying. He rode now through open woods, across little flower-scattered glades, till he came upon a spring. Flat on the ground, he drank deeply of the clear water, and looking about him, felt with a shock the beauty of the world. It came to him like a discovery; he had never realized it before, he concluded, and also, he had forgotten much. One could not sit in at high finance and keep track of such things. As he drank in the air, the scene, and the distant song of larks, he felt like a poker-player rising from a night-long table and coming forth from the pent atmosphere to taste the freshness of the morn.

At the base of the knolls he encountered a tumble-down stake-and-rider fence. From the look of it he judged it must be forty years old at least—the work of some first pioneer who had taken up the land when the days of gold had ended. The woods were very thick here, yet fairly clear of underbush, so that, while the blue sky was screened by the arched branches, he was able to ride beneath. He now found himself in a hook of several acres, where the oak and manzanita and madroño gave way to clusters of stately redwoods. Against the foot of a steep-sloped knoll he came upon a magnificent group of redwoods that seemed to have gathered about the tiny gurgling spring.

He halted his horse, for beside the spring uprose a wild California lily. It was a wonderful flower, growing there in the cathedral nave of lofty trees. At least eight feet in height, its stem rose straight and slender, green and bare, for two-thirds its length, and then burst into a shower of snow-white waxen bells. There were hundreds of these blossoms, all from the one stem, delicately poised and ethereally frail. Daylight had never seen anything like it. Slowly his gaze wandered from it to all that was about him. He took off his hat, with almost a vague religious feeling. This was different. No room for contempt and evil here. This was clean and fresh and beautiful— something he could respect. It was like a church. The atmosphere was one of holy calm. Here man felt the prompting of nobler things. Much of this and more was in Daylight's heart as he looked about him. But it was not a concept of his mind. He merely felt it without thinking about it at all.

On the steep incline above the spring grew tiny maiden-hair ferns, while higher up were larger ferns and brakes. Great, moss-covered trunks of fallen trees lay here and there, slowly sinking back and merging into the level of the forest mould. Beyond, in a slightly clearer space, wild grape and honeysuckle swung in green riot from gnarled old oak trees. A gray Douglas squirrel crept out on a branch and watched him. From somewhere came the distant knocking of a woodpecker. This sound did not disturb the hush and awe of the place. Quiet woods' noises belonged there and made the solitude complete. The tiny bubbling ripple of the spring and the gray flash of tree-squirrel were as yardsticks with which to measure the silence and motionless repose.

"Might be a million miles from anywhere," Daylight whispered to himself.

But ever his gaze returned to the wonderful lily beside the bubbling spring.

He tethered the horse and wandered on foot among the knolls. Their tops were crowned with century-old spruce trees, and their sides clothed with oaks and madroños and native holly. But to the perfect redwoods belonged the small but deep canyon that threaded its way among the knolls. Here he found no passage out for his horse, and he returned to the lily beside the spring. On foot, tripping, stumbling, leading the animal, he forced his way up the hillside. And ever the ferns carpeted the way of his feet, ever the forest climbed with him and arched overhead, and ever the clean joy and sweetness stole in upon his senses.

On the crest he came through an amazing thicket of velvet-trunked young madroños, and emerged on an open hillside that led down into a tiny valley. The sunshine was at first dazzling in its brightness, and he paused and rested, for he was panting from the exertion. Not of old had he known shortness of breath such as this, and muscles that so easily tired at a stiff climb. A tiny stream ran down the tiny valley through a tiny meadow that was carpeted knee-high with grass and blue and white nemophila. The hillside was covered with mariposa lilies and wild hyacinth, down through which his horse dropped slowly, with circumspect feet and reluctant gait.

Crossing the stream, Daylight followed a faint cattle-trail over a low, rocky hill and through a wine-wooded forest of manzanita, and emerged upon another tiny valley, down which filtered another spring-fed, meadow-bordered streamlet. A jack-rabbit bounded from a bush under his horse's nose, leaped the stream, and vanished up the opposite hillside of scrub-oak. Daylight watched it admiringly as he rode on to the head of the meadow. Here he startled up a many-pronged buck, that seemed to soar across the meadow, and to soar over the stake-and-rider fence, and, still soaring, disappeared in a friendly copse beyond.

Daylight's delight was unbounded. It seemed to him that he had never been so happy. His old woods' training was aroused, and he was keenly interested in everything—in the moss on the trees and branches; in the bunches of mistletoe hanging in the oaks; in the nest of a wood-rat; in the water-cress growing in the sheltered eddies of the little stream; in the butterflies drifting through the rifted sunshine and shadow; in the blue jays that flashed in splashes of gorgeous color across the forest aisles; in the tiny birds, like wrens, that hopped among the bushes and imitated certain minor quail-calls; and in the crimson-crested woodpecker that ceased its knocking and cocked its head on one side to survey him. Crossing the stream, he struck faint vestiges of a wood-road, used, evidently, a generation back, when the meadow had been cleared of its oaks. He found a hawk's nest on the lightning-shattered tipmost top of a six-foot redwood. And to complete it all, his horse stumbled upon several large broods of half-grown quail, and the air was filled with the thrum of their flight. He halted and watched the young ones "petrifying" and disappearing on the ground before his eyes, and listening to the anxious calls of the old ones hidden in the thickets.

"It sure beats country places and bungalows at Menlo Park," he communed aloud; "and if ever I get the hankering for country life, it's me for this every time."

The old wood-road led him to a clearing, where a dozen acres of grapes grew on wine-red soil. A cow-path, more trees and thickets, and he dropped down a hillside to the southeast exposure. Here, poised above a big forested canyon, and looking out upon Sonoma Valley, was a small farm-house. With its barn and outhouses it snuggled into a nook in the hillside, which protected it from west and north. It was the erosion from this hillside, he judged, that had formed the little level stretch of vegetable garden. The soil was fat and black, and there was water in plenty, for he saw several faucets running wide open.

Forgotten was the brickyard. Nobody was at home, but Daylight dismounted and ranged the vegetable garden, eating strawberries and green peas, inspecting the old adobe barn and the rusty plough and harrow, and rolling and smoking cigarettes while he watched the antics of several broods of young chickens and the mother hens. A foot-trail that led down the wall of the big canyon invited him, and he proceeded to follow it. A water-pipe, usually above ground, paralleled the trail, which he concluded led upstream to the bed of the creek. The wall of the canyon was several hundred feet from top to bottom, and so magnificent were the untouched trees that the place was plunged in perpetual shade. He measured with his eye spruces five and six feet in diameter and redwoods even larger. One such he passed, a twister that was at least ten or eleven feet through. The trail led straight to a small dam where was the intake for the pipe that watered the vegetable garden. Here, beside the stream, were alders and laurel trees, and he walked through fern-brakes higher than his head. Velvety moss was everywhere, out of which grew maiden-hair and gold-back ferns.

Save for the dam, it was a virgin wild. No axe had invaded, and the trees died only of old age and stress of winter storm. The huge trunks of those that had fallen lay moss-covered, slowly resolving back into the soil from which they sprang. Some had lain so long that they were quite gone, though their faint outlines, level with the mould, could still be seen. Others bridged the stream, and from beneath the bulk of one monster half a dozen younger trees, overthrown and crushed by the fall, growing out along the ground, still lived and prospered, their roots bathed by the stream, their up-shooting branches catching the sunlight through the gap that had been made in the forest roof.

Back at the farm-house, Daylight mounted and rode on away from the ranch and into the wilder canyons and steeper steeps beyond. Nothing could satisfy his holiday spirit now but the ascent of Sonoma Mountain. And here on the crest, three hours afterward, he emerged, tired and sweaty, garments torn and face and hands scratched, but with sparkling eyes and an unwonted zestfulness of expression. He felt the illicit pleasure of a schoolboy playing truant. The big gambling table of San Francisco seemed very far away. But there was more than illicit pleasure in his mood. It was as though he were going through a sort of cleansing bath. No room here for all the sordidness, meanness, and viciousness that filled the dirty pool of city existence. Without pondering in detail upon the matter at all, his sensations were of purification and uplift. Had he been asked to state how he felt, he would merely have said that he was having a good time; for he was unaware in his self-consciousness of the potent charm of nature that was percolating through his city-rotted body and brain—potent, in that he came of an abysmal past of wilderness dwellers, while he was himself coated with the thinnest rind of crowded civilization.

There were no houses in the summit of Sonoma Mountain, and, all alone under the azure California sky, he reined in on the southern edge of the peak. He saw open pasture country, intersected with wooden canyons, descending to the south and west from his feet, crease on crease and roll on roll, from lower level to lower level, to the floor of Petaluma Valley, flat as a billiard-table, a cardboard affair, all patches and squares of geometrical regularity where the fat freeholds were farmed. Beyond, to the west, rose range on range of mountains cuddling purple mists of atmosphere in their valleys; and still beyond, over the last range of all, he saw the silver sheen of the Pacific. Swinging his horse, he surveyed the west and north, from Santa Rosa to Mount St. Helena, and on to the east, across Sonoma Valley, to the chaparral-covered range that shut off the view of Napa Valley. Here, part way up the eastern wall of Sonoma Valley, in range of a line intersecting the little village of Glen Ellen, he made out a scar upon a hillside. His first thought was that it was the dump of a mine tunnel, but remembering that he was not in gold-bearing country, he dismissed the scar from his mind and continued the circle of his survey to the southeast, where, across the waters of San Pablo Bay, he could see, sharp and distant, the twin peaks of Mount Diablo. To the south was Mount Tamalpais, and, yes, he was right, fifty miles away, where the draughty winds of the Pacific blew in the Golden Gate, the smoke of San Francisco made a low-lying haze against the sky.

"I ain't seen so much country all at once in many a day," he thought aloud.

He was loath to depart, and it was not for an hour that he was able to tear himself away and take the descent of the mountain. Working out a new route just for the fun of it, late afternoon was upon him when he arrived back at the wooded knolls. Here, on the top of one of them, his keen eyes caught a glimpse of a shade of green sharply differentiated from any he had seen all day. Studying it for a minute, he concluded that it was composed of three cypress trees, and he knew that nothing else than the hand of man could have planted them there. Impelled by curiosity purely boyish, he

57

made up his mind to investigate. So densely wooded was the knoll, and so steep, that he had to dismount and go up on foot, at times even on hands and knees struggling hard to force a way through the thicker underbrush. He came out abruptly upon the cypresses. They were enclosed in a small square of ancient fence; the pickets he could plainly see had been hewn and sharpened by hand. Inside were the mounds of two children's graves. Two wooden headboards, likewise hand-hewn, told the story: *Little David, born 1855, died 1859;* and *Little Lily, born 1853, died 1860.*

"The poor little kids," Daylight muttered.

The graves showed signs of recent care. Withered bouquets of wild flowers were on the mounds, and the lettering on the headboards was freshly painted. Guided by these clews, Daylight cast about for a trail, and found one leading down the side opposite to his ascent. Circling the base of the knoll, he picked up with his horse and rode on to the farm-house. Smoke was rising from the chimney, and he was quickly in conversation with a nervous, slender young man, who, he learned, was only a tenant on the ranch. How large was it? A matter of one hundred and eighty acres, though it seemed much larger. This was because it was so irregularly shaped. Yes, it included the clay-pit and all the knolls, and its boundary that ran along the big canyon was over a mile long.

"You see," the young man said, "it was so rough and broken that when they began to farm this country the farmers bought in the good land to the edge of it. That's why its boundaries are all gouged and jagged."

Oh, yes, he and his wife managed to scratch a living without working too hard. They didn't have to pay much rent. Hillard, the owner, depended on the income from the clay-pit. Hillard was well off, and had big ranches and vineyards down on the flat of the valley. The brickyard paid ten cents a cubic yard for the clay. As for the rest of the ranch, the land was good in patches, where it was cleared, like the vegetable garden and the vineyard, but the rest of it was too much up-and-down.

"You're not a farmer," Daylight said.

The young man laughed and shook his head.

"No; I'm a telegraph operator. But the wife and I decided to take a two years' vacation, and . . . here we are. But the time's about up. I'm going back into the office this fall after I get the grapes off."

Yes, there were about eleven acres in the vineyard—wine grapes. The price was usually good. He grew most of what they ate. If he owned the place, he'd clear a patch of land on the side-hill above the vineyard and plant a small home orchard. The soil was good.

There was plenty of pasturage all over the ranch, and there were several cleared patches, amounting to about fifteen acres in all, where he grew as fine mountain hay as could be found. It sold for three to five dollars more a ton than the rank-stalked valley hay.

As Daylight listened, there came to him a sudden envy of this young fellow living right in the midst of all this which Daylight had travelled through the last few hours.

"What in thunder are you going back to the telegraph office for?" he demanded.

The young man smiled with a certain wistfulness.

"Because we can't get ahead here . . ." (he hesitated an instant), "and because there are added expenses coming. The rent, small as it is, counts; and besides, I'm not strong enough to effectually farm the place. If I owned it, or if I were a real husky like you, I'd ask nothing better. Nor would the wife." Again the wistful smile hovered on his face. "You see, we're country born, and after bucking with cities for a few years, we kind of feel we like the country best. We've planned to get ahead, though, and then some day we'll buy a patch of land and stay with it."

The graves of the children? Yes, he had relettered them and hoed the weeds out. It had become the custom. Whoever lived on the ranch did that. For years, the story ran, the father and mother had returned each summer to the graves. But there had come a time when they came no more, and then old Hillard started the custom. The scar across the valley? An old mine. It had never paid. The men had worked on it, off and on, for years, for the indication had been good. But that was years and years ago. No paying mine had ever been struck in the valley, though there had been no end of prospect-holes put down, and there had been a sort of rush there thirty years back.

A frail-looking young woman came to the door to call the young man to supper. Daylight's first thought was that city living had not agreed with her. And then he noted the slight tan and healthy glow that seemed added to her face, and he decided that the country was the place for her. Declining an invitation to supper, he rode on for Glen Ellen, sitting slack-kneed in the saddle and softly humming forgotten songs. He dropped down the rough, winding road, through oak-covered pasture, with here and there thickets of manzanita and vistas of open glades. He listened greedily to the quail calling, and laughed outright, once, in sheer joy, at a tiny chipmunk that fled scolding up a bank, slipping on the crumbly surface and falling down, then dashing across the road under his horse's nose and, still scolding, scrambling up a protecting oak.

Daylight could not persuade himself to keep to the travelled roads that day, and another cut across country to Glen Ellen brought him upon a canyon that so blocked his way that he was glad to follow a friendly cow-path. This led him to a small frame cabin. The doors and windows were open, and a cat was nursing a litter of kittens in the doorway, but no one seemed at home. He descended the trail that evidently crossed the canyon. Part way down, he met an old man coming up through the sunset. In his hand he carried a pail of foamy milk. He wore no hat, and in his face, framed with snow-white hair and beard, was the ruddy glow and content of the passing summer day. Daylight thought that he had never seen so contented-looking a being.

"How old are you, daddy?" he queried.

"Eighty-four," was the reply. "Yes, sirree, eighty-four, and spryer than most."

"You must a' taken good care of yourself," Daylight suggested.

"I don't know about that. I ain't loafed none. I walked across the Plains with an ox-team and fit Injuns in '51, and I was a family man then with seven youngsters. I reckon I was as old then as you are now, or pretty nigh on to it."

"Don't you find it lonely here?"

The old man shifted the pail of milk and reflected.

"That all depends," he said oracularly. "I ain't never been lonely except when the old wife died. Some fellers are lonely in a crowd, and I'm one of them. That's the only time I'm lonely, is when I go to 'Frisco. But I don't go no more, thank you 'most to death. This is good enough for me. I've ben right here in this valley since '54— one of the first settlers after the Spaniards."

Daylight started his horse, saying:—

"Well, good night, daddy. Stick with it. You got all the young bloods skinned, and I guess you've sure buried a mighty sight of them."

The old man chuckled, and Daylight rode on, singularly at peace with himself and all the world. It seemed that the old contentment of trail and camp he had known on the Yukon had come back to him. He could not shake from his eyes the picture of the old pioneer coming up the trail through the sunset light. He was certainly going some for eighty-four. The thought of following his example entered Daylight's mind, but the big game of San Francisco vetoed the idea.

"Well, anyway," he decided, "when I get old and quit the game, I'll settle down in a place something like this, and the city can go to hell."

Instead of returning to the city on Monday, Daylight rented the butcher's horse for another day and crossed the bed of the valley to its eastern hills to look at the mine. It was dryer and rockier here than where he had been the day before, and the ascending slopes supported mainly chaparral—scrubby and dense and impossible to penetrate on horseback. But in the canyons water was plentiful and also a luxuriant forest growth. The mine was an abandoned affair, but he enjoyed the half-hour's scramble around. He had had experience in quartz-mining before he went to Alaska, and he enjoyed the recrudescence of his old wisdom in such matters. The story was simple to him: good prospects that warranted the starting of the tunnel into the side-hill; the three months' work and the getting short of money; the lay-off while the men went away and got jobs; then the return and a new stretch of work, with the "pay" ever luring and ever receding into the mountain, until after years of hope, the men had given up and vanished. Most likely they were dead by now, Daylight thought, as he turned in the saddle and looked back across the canyon at the ancient dump and dark mouth of the tunnel.

As on the previous day, just for the joy of it, he followed cattle-trails at haphazard and worked his way up toward the summits. Coming out on a wagon road that led upward, he followed it for several miles, emerging in a small, mountain-encircled valley, where half a dozen poor ranchers farmed the wine grapes on the steep slopes. Beyond, the road pitched upward. Dense chaparral covered the exposed hillsides, but in the creases of the canyons huge spruce trees grew, and wild oats and flowers.

Half an hour later, sheltering under the summits themselves, he came out on a clearing. Here and there, in irregular patches where the steep and the soil favored, wine grapes were growing. Daylight could see that it had been a stiff struggle, and that wild nature showed fresh signs of winning—chaparral that had invaded the clearings; patches and parts of patches of vineyard, unpruned, grassgrown, and abandoned; and everywhere old stake-and-rider fences vainly striving to remain intact. Here, at a small farm-house surrounded by large outbuildings, the road ended. Beyond, the chaparral blocked the way.

He came upon an old woman forking manure in the barnyard, and reined in by the fence.

"Hello, mother," was his greeting; "ain't you got ary men-folk around to do that for you?"

She leaned on her pitchfork, hitched her skirt in at the waist, and regarded him cheerfully. He saw that her toil-worn, weather-exposed hands were like a man's, calloused, large-knuckled, and gnarled, and that her stockingless feet were thrust into heavy man's brogans.

"Nary a man," she answered. "And where be you from, and all the way up here? Won't you stop and hitch and have a glass of wine?"

Striding clumsily but efficiently, like a laboring-man, she led him into the largest building, where Daylight saw a hand-press and all the paraphernalia on a small scale for the making of wine. It was too far and too bad a road to haul the grapes to the valley wineries, she explained, and so they were compelled to do it themselves. "They," he learned, were she and her daughter, the latter a widow of forty-odd. It had been easier before the grandson died and before he went away to fight savages in the Philippines. He had died out there in battle.

Daylight drank a full tumbler of excellent Riesling, talked a few minutes, and accounted for a second tumbler. Yes, they just managed not to starve. Her husband and she had taken up this government land in '57 and cleared it and farmed it ever since, until he died, when she had carried it on. It actually didn't pay for the toil, but what were they to do? There was the wine trust, and wine was down. That Riesling? She delivered it to the railroad down in the valley for twenty-two cents a gallon. And it was a long haul. It took a day for the round trip. Her daughter was gone now with a load.

Daylight knew that in the hotels, Riesling, not quite so good even, was charged for at from a dollar and a half to two dollars a quart. And she got twenty-two cents a gallon. That was the game. She was one of the stupid lowly, she and her people before her—the ones that did the work, drove their oxen across the Plains, cleared and broke the virgin land, toiled all days and all hours, paid their taxes, and sent their sons and grandsons out to fight and die for the flag that gave them such ample protection that they were able to sell their wine for twenty-two cents. The same wine was served to him at the St. Francis for two dollars a quart, or eight dollars a short gallon. That was it.

Between her and her hand-press on the mountain clearing and him ordering his wine in the hotel was a difference of seven dollars and seventy-eight cents. A clique of sleek men in the city got between her and him to just about that amount. And, besides them, there was a horde of others that took their whack. They called it railroading, high finance, banking, wholesaling, real estate, and such things, but the point was that they got it, while she got what was left— twenty-two cents. Oh, well, a sucker was born every minute, he sighed to himself, and nobody was to blame; it was all a game, and only a few could win, but it was damned hard on the suckers.

"How old are you, mother?" he asked.

"Seventy-nine come next January."

"Worked pretty hard, I suppose?"

"Sence I was seven. I was bound out in Michigan state until I was woman-grown. Then I married, and I reckon the work got harder and harder."

"When are you going to take a rest?"

She looked at him, as though she chose to think his question facetious, and did not reply.

"Do you believe in God?"

She nodded her head.

"Then you get it all back," he assured her; but in his heart he was wondering about God, that allowed so many suckers to be born and that did not break up the gambling game by which they were robbed from the cradle to the grave.

"How much of that Riesling you got?"

She ran her eyes over the casks and calculated. "Just short of eight hundred gallons."

He wondered what he could do with all of it, and speculated as to whom he could give it away.

"What would you do if you got a dollar a gallon for it?" he asked.

"Drop dead, I suppose."

"No; speaking seriously."

"Get me some false teeth, shingle the house, and buy a new wagon. The road's mighty hard on wagons."

"And after that?"

"Buy me a coffin."

"Well, they're yours, mother, coffin and all."

She looked her incredulity.

"No; I mean it. And there's fifty to bind the bargain. Never mind the receipt. It's the rich ones that need watching, their memories being so infernal short, you know. Here's my address. You've got to deliver it to the railroad. And now, show me the way out of here. I want to get up to the top."

On through the chaparral he went, following faint cattle-trails and working slowly upward till he came out on the divide and gazed down into Napa Valley and back across to Sonoma Mountain.

"A sweet land," he muttered, "an almighty sweet land."

Circling around to the right and dropping down along the cattle-trails, he quested for another way back to Sonoma Valley; but the cattle-trails seemed to fade out, and the chaparral to grow thicker with a deliberate viciousness, and even when he won through in places, the canyon and small feeders were too precipitous for his horse, and turned him back. But there was no irritation about it. He enjoyed it all, for he was back at his old game of bucking nature. Late in the afternoon he broke through, and followed a well-defined trail down a dry canyon. Here he got a fresh thrill. He had heard the baying of the hound some minutes before, and suddenly, across the bare face of the hill above him, he saw a large buck in flight. And not far behind came the deer-hound, a magnificent animal. Daylight sat tense in his saddle and watched until they disappeared, his breath just a trifle shorter, as if he, too, were in the chase, his nostrils distended, and in his bones the old hunting ache and memories of the days before he came to live in cities.

The dry canyon gave place to one with a slender ribbon of running water. The trail ran into a wood-road, and the wood-road emerged across a small flat upon a slightly travelled county road. There were no farms in this immediate section, and no houses. The soil was meagre, the bed-rock either close to the surface or constituting the surface itself. Manzanita and scrub-oak, however, flourished and walled the road on either side with a jungle growth. And out a runway through this growth a man suddenly scuttled in a way that reminded Daylight of a rabbit.

He was a little man, in patched overalls; bareheaded, with a cotton shirt open at the throat and down the chest. The sun was ruddy-brown in his face, and by it his sandy hair was bleached on the ends to peroxide blonde. He signed to Daylight to halt, and held up a letter.

"If you're going to town, I'd be obliged if you mail this," he said.

"I sure will." Daylight put it into his coat pocket. "Do you live hereabouts, stranger?"

But the little man did not answer. He was gazing at Daylight in a surprised and steadfast fashion.

"I know you," the little man announced. "You're Elam Harnish—Burning Daylight, the papers call you. Am I right?"

Daylight nodded.

"But what under the sun are you doing here in the chaparral?"

Daylight grinned as he answered, "Drumming up trade for a free rural delivery route."

"Well, I'm glad I wrote that letter this afternoon," the little man went on, "or else I'd have missed seeing you. I've seen your photo in the papers many a time, and I've a good memory for faces. I recognized you at once. My name's Ferguson."

"Do you live hereabouts?" Daylight repeated his query.

"Oh, yes. I've got a little shack back here in the bush a hundred yards, and a pretty spring, and a few fruit trees and berry bushes. Come in and take a look. And that spring is a dandy. You never tasted water like it. Come in and try it."

Walking and leading his horse, Daylight followed the quick-stepping, eager little man through the green tunnel and emerged abruptly upon the clearing, if clearing it might be called, where wild nature and man's earth-scratching were inextricably blended. It was a tiny nook in the hills, protected by the steep walls of a canyon mouth. Here were several large oaks, evidencing a richer soil. The erosion of ages from the hillside had slowly formed this deposit of fat earth. Under the oaks, almost buried in them, stood a rough, unpainted cabin, the wide veranda of which, with chairs and hammocks, advertised an out-of-doors bedchamber. Daylight's keen eyes took in everything. The clearing was irregular, following the patches of the best soil, and every fruit tree and berry bush, and even each vegetable plant, had the water personally conducted to it. The tiny irrigation channels were everywhere, and along some of them the water was running.

Ferguson looked eagerly into his visitor's face for signs of approbation.

"What do you think of it, eh?"

"Hand-reared and manicured, every blessed tree," Daylight laughed, but the joy and satisfaction that shone in his eyes contented the little man.

"Why, d'ye know, I know every one of those trees as if they were sons of mine. I planted them, nursed them, fed them, and brought them up. Come on and peep at the spring."

"It's sure a hummer," was Daylight's verdict, after due inspection and sampling, as they turned back for the house.

The interior was a surprise. The cooking being done in the small, lean-to kitchen, the whole cabin formed a large living room. A great table in the middle was comfortably littered with books and magazines. All the available wall space, from floor to ceiling, was occupied by filled bookshelves. It seemed to Daylight that he had never seen so many books assembled in one place. Skins of wildcat, 'coon, and deer lay about on the pine-board floor.

"Shot them myself, and tanned them, too," Ferguson proudly asserted.

The crowning feature of the room was a huge fireplace of rough stones and boulders.

"Built it myself," Ferguson proclaimed, "and, by God, she drew! Never a wisp of smoke anywhere save in the appointed channel, and that during the big southeasters, too."

Daylight found himself charmed and made curious by the little man. Why was he hiding away here in the chaparral, he and his books? He was nobody's fool, anybody could see that. Then why? The whole affair had a tinge of adventure, and Daylight accepted an invitation to supper, half prepared to find his host a raw-fruit-and-nut-eater, or some similar sort of health faddist. At table, while eating rice and jack-rabbit curry (the latter shot by Ferguson), they talked it over, and Daylight found the little man had no food "views." He ate whatever he liked, and all he wanted, avoiding only such combinations that experience had taught him disagreed with his digestion.

Next, Daylight surmised that he might be touched with religion; but, quest about as he would, in a conversation covering the most divergent topics, he could find no hint of queerness or unusualness. So it was, when between them they had washed and wiped the dishes and put them away, and had settled down to a comfortable smoke, that Daylight put his question.

"Look here, Ferguson. Ever since we got together, I've been casting about to find out what's wrong with you, to locate a screw loose somewhere, but I'll be danged if I've succeeded. What are you doing here, anyway? What made you come here? What were you doing for a living before you came here? Go ahead and elucidate yourself."

Ferguson frankly showed his pleasure at the questions.

"First of all," he began, "the doctors wound up by losing all hope for me. Gave me a few months at best, and that, after a course in sanatoriums and a trip to Europe and another to Hawaii. They tried electricity, and forced feeding, and fasting. I was a graduate of about everything in the curriculum. They kept me poor with their bills, while I went from bad to worse. The trouble with me was twofold: first, I was a born weakling; and next, I was living unnaturally—too much work, and responsibility, and strain. I was managing editor of the *Times-Tribune*—"

Daylight gasped mentally, for the *Times-Tribune* was the biggest and most influential paper in San Francisco, and always had been so.

"—and I wasn't strong enough for the strain. Of course my body went back on me, and my mind, too, for that matter. It had to be bolstered up with whiskey, which wasn't good for it any more than was the living in clubs and hotels good for my stomach and the rest of me. That was what ailed me; I was living all wrong."

He shrugged his shoulders and drew at his pipe.

"When the doctors gave me up, I wound up my affairs and gave the doctors up. That was fifteen years ago. I'd been hunting through here when I was a boy, on vacations from college, and when I was all down and out it seemed a yearning came to me to go back to the country. So I quit, quit everything, absolutely, and came to live in the Valley of the Moon—that's the Indian name, you know, for Sonoma Valley. I lived in the lean-to the first year; then I built the cabin and sent for my books. I never knew what happiness was before, nor health. Look at me now and dare to tell me that I look forty-seven."

"I wouldn't give a day over forty," Daylight confessed.

"Yet the day I came here I looked nearer sixty, and that was fifteen years ago."

They talked along, and Daylight looked at the world from new angles. Here was a man, neither bitter nor cynical, who laughed at the city-dwellers and called them lunatics; a man who did not care for money, and in whom the lust for power had long since died. As for the friendship of the city-dwellers, his host spoke in no uncertain terms.

"What did they do, all the chaps I knew, the chaps in the clubs, with whom I'd been cheek by jowl for heaven knows how long? I was not beholden to them for anything, and when I slipped out there was not one of them to drop me a line and say, 'How are you, old man? Anything I can do for you?' For several weeks it was: 'What's become of Ferguson?' After that I became a reminiscence and a memory. Yet every last one of them knew I had nothing but my salary and that I'd always lived a lap ahead of it."

"But what do you do now?" was Daylight's query. "You must need cash to buy clothes and magazines?"

"A week's work or a month's work, now and again, ploughing in the winter, or picking grapes in the fall, and there's always odd jobs with the farmers through the summer. I don't need much, so I don't have to work much. Most of my time I spend fooling around the place. I could do hackwork for the magazines and newspapers; but I prefer the ploughing and the grape picking. Just look at me and you can see why. I'm hard as rocks. And I like the work. But I tell you a chap's got to break in to it. It's a great thing when he's learned to pick grapes a whole long day and come home at the end of it with that tired happy feeling, instead of being in a state of physical collapse. That fireplace—those big stones—I was soft, then, a little, anemic, alcoholic degenerate, with the spunk of a rabbit and about one per cent as much stamina, and some of those big stones nearly broke my back and my heart. But I persevered, and used my body in the way Nature intended it should be used—not bending over a desk and swilling whiskey . . . and, well, here I am, a better man for it, and there's the fireplace, fine and dandy, eh?

"And now tell me about the Klondike, and how you turned San Francisco upside down with that last raid of yours. You're a bonny fighter, you know, and you touch my imagination, though my cooler reason tells me that you are a lunatic like the rest. The lust for power! It's a dreadful affliction. Why didn't you stay in your Klondike? Or why don't you clear out and live a natural life, for instance, like mine? You see, I can ask questions, too. Now you talk and let me listen for a while."

It was not until ten o'clock that Daylight parted from Ferguson. As he rode along through the starlight, the idea came to him of buying the ranch on the other side of the valley. There was no thought in his mind of ever intending to live on it. His game was in San Francisco. But he liked the ranch, and as soon as he got back to the office he would open up negotiations with Hillard. Besides, the ranch included the clay-pit, and it would give him the whip-hand over Holdsworthy if he ever tried to cut up any didoes.

5.

All Gold Canyon

In August 1898, when Jack London returned home with less than five dollars worth of gold after a year of prospecting and hardship in the Klondike, the golden shores of California must have been a welcome sight to the weary adventurer. But he soon faced the responsibility of earning enough money to help support his family. Work of any kind, however, was practically impossible to find at the time.

Little has surfaced about this period of his life, but it is known that he went to Yosemite with a group of friends. After witnessing the awesome wonders of the famed valley, he and another young man from his party ventured off into the Mother Lode country of the Sierra Nevadas. Here they camped out under the pines and stars, prospected, and wandered about the countryside for several weeks. Undoubtedly they encountered a few old-timers—prospectors who lingered on, picking away at the earth with hopes of striking it rich, nearly fifty years after the height of California's famed gold rush.

Later, using this California background and his mining experiences among a host of "sourdoughs" and "chechaquos" in the Klondike, London fashioned the story "All Gold Canyon," in which he depicted an unspoiled wilderness quite out of harmony with the destructive nature of man, who becomes its spoiler.

This story is certainly reminiscent of the best of Bret Harte's tales of the Gold Rush era. But London's theme and descriptive brilliance surpass Harte's mythical West, which often became a scenario of stock characters, places, and events that never existed in California's El Dorado.

Jack London in the summer of 1898, when he went "mining, prospecting, and wandering through the Sierra Nevadas" shortly after his return
from the Klondike. *Photograph courtesy of Arnold and Virginia Applegarth*

ALL GOLD CANYON

IT WAS THE GREEN HEART OF THE CANYON, WHERE THE walls swerved back from the rigid plain and relieved their harshness of line by making a little sheltered nook and filling it to the brim with sweetness and roundness and softness. Here all things rested. Even the narrow stream ceased its turbulent down-rush long enough to form a quiet pool. Knee-deep in the water, with drooping head and half-shut eyes, drowsed a red-coated, many-antlered buck.

On one side, beginning at the very lip of the pool, was a tiny meadow, a cool, resilient surface of green that extended to the base of the frowning wall. Beyond the pool a gentle slope of earth ran up and up to meet the opposing wall. Fine grass covered the slope— grass that was spangled with flowers, with here and there patches of color, orange and purple and golden. Below, the canyon was shut in. There was no view. The walls leaned together abruptly and the canyon ended in a chaos of rocks, moss-covered and hidden by a green screen of vines and creepers and boughs of trees. Up the canyon rose far hills and peaks, the big foothills, pine-covered and remote. And far beyond, like clouds upon the border of the sky, towered minarets of white, where the Sierra's eternal snows flashed austerely the blazes of the sun.

There was no dust in the canyon. The leaves and flowers were clean and virginal. The grass was young velvet. Over the pool three cottonwoods sent their snowy fluffs fluttering down the quiet air. On the slope the blossoms of the wine-wooded manzanita filled the air with springtime odors, while the leaves, wise with experience, were already beginning their vertical twist against the coming aridity of summer. In the open spaces on the slope, beyond the farthest shadow-reach of the manzanita, poised the mariposa lilies, like so many flights of jewelled moths suddenly arrested and on the verge of trembling into flight again. Here and there that woods harlequin, the madrone, permitting itself to be caught in the act of changing its pea-green trunk to madder-red, breathed its fragrance into the air from great clusters of waxen bells. Creamy white were these bells, shaped like lilies-of-the-valley, with the sweetness of perfume that is of the springtime.

There was not a sigh of wind. The air was drowsy with its weight of perfume. It was a sweetness that would have been cloying had the air been heavy and humid. But the air was sharp and thin. It was as starlight transmuted into atmosphere, shot through and warmed by sunshine, and flower-drenched with sweetness.

An occasional butterfly drifted in and out through the patches of light and shade. And from all about rose the low and sleepy hum of mountain bees—feasting Sybarites that jostled one another good-naturedly at the board, nor found time for rough discourtesy. So quietly did the little stream drip and ripple its way through the canyon that it spoke only in faint and occasional gurgles. The voice of the stream was as a drowsy whisper, ever interrupted by dozings and silences, ever lifted again in the awakenings.

The motion of all things was a drifting in the heart of the canyon. Sunshine and butterflies drifted in and out among the trees. The hum of the bees and the whisper of the stream were a drifting of sound. And the drifting sound and drifting color seemed to weave together in the making of a delicate and intangible fabric which was the spirit of the place. It was a spirit of peace that was not of death, but of smooth-pulsing life, of quietude that was not silence, of movement that was not action, of repose that was quick with existence without being violent with struggle and travail. The spirit of the place was the spirit of the peace of the living, somnolent with the easement and contents of prosperity, and undisturbed by rumors of far wars.

The red-coated, many-antlered buck acknowledged the lordship of the spirit of the place and dozed knee-deep in the cool, shaded pool. There seemed no flies to vex him and he was languid with rest. Sometimes his ears moved when the stream awoke and whispered; but they moved lazily, with foreknowledge that it was merely the stream grown garrulous at discovery that it had slept.

But there came a time when the buck's ears lifted and tensed with swift eagerness for sound. His head was turned down the canyon. His sensitive, quivering nostrils scented the air. His eyes could not pierce the green screen through which the stream rippled away, but to his ears came the voice of a man. It was a steady, monotonous, singsong voice. Once the buck heard the harsh clash of metal upon rock. At the sound he snorted with a sudden start that jerked him through the air from water to meadow, and his feet sank into the young velvet, while he pricked his ears and again scented the air. Then he stole across the tiny meadow, pausing once and again to listen, and faded away out of the canyon like a wraith, soft-footed and without sound.

The clash of steel-shod soles against the rocks began to be heard, and the man's voice grew louder. It was raised in a sort of chant and became distinct with nearness, so that the words could be heard:

"Tu'n around an' tu'n yo' face
Untoe them sweet hills of grace
    (D' pow'rs of sin yo' am scornin'!).
Look about an' look aroun',
Fling yo' sin-pack on d' groun'
    (Yo' will meet wid d' Lord in d' mornin'!)."

A sound of scrambling accompanied the song, and the spirit of the place fled away on the heels of the red-coated buck. The green screen was burst asunder, and a man peered out at the meadow and the pool and the sloping side-hill. He was a deliberate sort of man. He took in the scene with one embracing glance, then ran his eyes over the details to verify the general impression. Then, and not until then, did he open his mouth in vivid and solemn approval:

"Smoke of life an' snakes of purgatory! Will you just look at that! Wood an' water an' grass an' a side-hill! A pocket-hunter's delight an' a cayuse's paradise! Cool green for tired eyes! Pink pills for pale people ain't in it. A secret pasture for prospectors and a resting-place for tired burros, by damn!"

He was a sandy-complexioned man in whose face geniality and humor seemed the salient characteristics. It was a mobile face, quick-changing to inward mood and thought. Thinking was in him a visible process. Ideas chased across his face like wind-flaws across the surface of a lake. His hair, sparse and unkempt of growth, was as indeterminate and colorless as his complexion. It would seem that all the color of his frame had gone into his eyes, for they were startlingly blue. Also, they were laughing and merry eyes, within them much of the naïveté and wonder of the child; and yet, in an unassertive way, they contained much of calm self-reliance and strength of purpose founded upon self-experience and experience of the world.

From out the screen of vines and creepers he flung ahead of him a miner's pick and shovel and gold-pan. Then he crawled out himself into the open. He was clad in faded overalls and black cotton shirt, with hobnailed brogans on his feet, and on his head a hat whose shapelessness and stains advertised the rough usage of wind and rain and sun and camp-smoke. He stood erect, seeing wide-eyed the secrecy of the scene and sensuously inhaling the warm, sweet breath of the canyon-garden through nostrils that dilated and quivered with delight. His eyes narrowed to laughing slits of blue, his face wreathed itself in joy, and his mouth curled in a smile as he cried aloud:

"Jumping dandelions and happy hollyhocks, but that smells good to me! Talk about your attar o' roses an' cologne factories! They ain't in it!"

He had the habit of soliloquy. His quick-changing facial expressions might tell every thought and mood, but the tongue, perforce, ran hard after, repeating, like a second Boswell.

The man lay down on the lip of the pool and drank long and deep of its water. "Tastes good to me," he murmured, lifting his head and gazing across the pool at the side-hill, while he wiped his mouth with the back of his hand. The side-hill attracted his attention. Still lying on his stomach, he studied the hill formation long and carefully. It was a practised eye that travelled up the slope to the crumbling canyon-wall and back and down again to the edge of the pool. He scrambled to his feet and favored the side-hill with a second survey.

"Looks good to me," he concluded, picking up his pick and shovel and gold-pan.

He crossed the stream below the pool, stepping agilely from stone to stone. Where the side-hill touched the water he dug up a shovelful of dirt and put it into the gold-pan. He squatted down, holding the pan in his two hands, and partly immersing it in the stream. Then he imparted to the pan a deft circular motion that sent the water sluicing in and out through the dirt and gravel. The larger and the lighter particles worked to the surface, and these, by a skillful dipping movement of the pan, he spilled out and over the edge. Occasionally, to expedite matters, he rested the pan and with his fingers raked out the large pebbles and pieces of rock.

The contents of the pan diminished rapidly until only fine dirt and the smallest bits of gravel remained. At this stage he began to work very deliberately and carefully. It was fine washing, and he washed fine and finer, with a keen scrutiny and delicate and fastidious touch. At last the pan seemed empty of everything but water; but with a quick semicircular flirt that sent the water flying over the shallow rim into the stream, he disclosed a layer of black sand on the bottom of the pan. So thin was this layer that it was like a streak of paint. He examined it closely. In the midst of it was a tiny golden speck. He dribbled a little water in over the depressed edge of the pan. With a quick flirt he sent the water sluicing across the bottom, turning the grains of black sand over and over. A second tiny golden speck rewarded his effort.

The washing had now become very fine—fine beyond all need of ordinary placer-mining. He worked the black sand, a small portion at a time, up the shallow rim of the pan. Each small portion he examined sharply, so that his eyes saw every grain of it before he allowed it to slide over the edge and away. Jealously, bit by bit, he let the black sand slip away. A golden speck, no larger than a pinpoint, appeared on the rim, and by his manipulation of the water it returned to the bottom of the pan. And in such fashion another speck was disclosed, and another. Great was his care of them. Like a shepherd he herded his flock of golden specks so that not one should be lost. At last, of the pan of dirt nothing remained but his golden herd. He counted it, and then, after all his labor, sent it flying out of the pan with one final swirl of water.

But his blue eyes were shining with desire as he rose to his feet. "Seven," he muttered aloud, asserting the sum of the specks for which he had toiled so hard and which he had so wantonly thrown away. "Seven," he repeated, with the emphasis of one trying to impress a number on his memory.

He stood still a long while, surveying the hillside. In his eyes was a curiosity, new-aroused and burning. There was an exultance about his bearing and a keenness like that of a hunting animal catching the fresh scent of game.

He moved down the stream a few steps and took a second panful of dirt.

Again came the careful washing, the jealous herding of the golden specks, and the wantonness with which he sent them flying into the stream when he had counted their number.

"Five," he muttered, and repeated, "five."

He could not forbear another survey of the hill before filling the pan farther down the stream. His golden herds diminished. "Four, three, two, two, one," were his memory-tabulations as he moved down the stream. When but one speck of gold rewarded his washing, he stopped and built a fire of dry twigs. Into this he thrust the gold-pan and burned it till it was blue-black. He held up the pan and examined it critically. Then he nodded approbation. Against such a color-background he could defy the tiniest yellow speck to elude him.

Still moving down the stream, he panned again. A single speck was his reward. A third pan contained no gold at all. Not satisfied with this, he panned three times again, taking his shovels of dirt within a foot of one another. Each pan proved empty of gold, and the fact, instead of discouraging him, seemed to give him satisfaction. His elation increased with each barren washing, until he arose, exclaiming jubilantly:

"If it ain't the real thing, may God knock off my head with sour apples!"

Returning to where he had started operations, he began to pan up the stream. At first his golden herds increased—increased prodigiously. "Fourteen, eighteen, twenty-one, twenty-six," ran his memory-tabulations. Just above the pool he struck his richest pan— thirty-five colors.

"Almost enough to save," he remarked regretfully as he allowed the water to sweep them away.

The sun climbed to the top of the sky. The man worked on. Pan by pan, he went up the stream, the tally of results steadily decreasing.

"It's just booful, the way it peters out," he exulted when a shovelful of dirt contained no more than a single speck of gold.

And when no specks at all were found in several pans, he straightened up and favored the hillside with a confident glance.

"Ah, ha! Mr. Pocket!" he cried out, as though to an auditor hidden somewhere above him beneath the surface of the slope. "Ah, ha! Mr. Pocket! I'm a-comin', I'm a-comin', an' I'm shorely gwine to get yer! You heah me, Mr. Pocket? I'm gwine to get yer as shore as punkins ain't cauliflowers!"

He turned and flung a measuring glance at the sun poised above him in the azure of the cloudless sky. Then he went down the canyon, following the line of shovel-holes he had made in filling the pans. He crossed the stream below the pool and disappeared through the green screen. There was little opportunity for the spirit of the place to return with its quietude and repose, for the man's voice, raised in ragtime song, still dominated the canyon with possession.

After a time, with a greater clashing of steel-shod feet on rock, he returned. The green screen was tremendously agitated. It surged back and forth in the throes of a struggle. There was a loud grating and clanging of metal. The man's voice leaped to a higher pitch and was sharp with imperativeness. A large body plunged and panted. There was a snapping and ripping and rending, and amid a shower of falling leaves a horse burst through the screen. On its back was a pack, and from this trailed broken vines and torn creepers. The animal gazed with astonished eyes at the scene into which it had been precipitated, then dropped its head to the grass and began contentedly to graze. A second horse scrambled into view, slipping once on the mossy rocks and regaining equilibrium when its hoofs sank into the yielding surface of the meadow. It was riderless, though on its back was a high-horned Mexican saddle, scarred and discolored by long usage.

The man brought up the rear. He threw off pack and saddle, with an eye to camp location, and gave the animals their freedom to graze. He unpacked his food and got out frying pan and coffee pot. He gathered an armful of dry wood, and with a few stones made a place for his fire.

"My!" he said, "but I've got an appetite. I could scoff iron-fillings an' horseshoe nails an' thank you kindly, ma'am, for a second helpin'."

He straightened up, and, while he reached for matches in the pocket of his overalls, his eyes travelled across the pool to the sidehill. His fingers had clutched the match-box, but they relaxed their hold and the hand came out empty. The man wavered perceptibly. He looked at his preparations for cooking and he looked at the hill.

"Guess I'll take another whack at her," he concluded, starting to cross the stream.

"They ain't no sense in it, I know," he mumbled apologetically. "But keepin' grub back an hour ain't goin' to hurt none, I reckon."

A few feet back from his first line of test-pans he started a second line. The sun dropped down the western sky, the shadows lengthened, but the man worked on. He began a third line of test-pans. He was cross-cutting the hillside, line by line, as he ascended. The centre of each line produced the richest pans, while the ends came where no colors showed in the pan. And as he ascended the hillside the lines grew perceptibly shorter. The regularity with which their length diminished served to indicate that somewhere up the slope the last line would be so short as to have scarcely length at all, and that beyond could come only a point. The design was growing into an inverted "V." The converging sides of this "V" marked the boundaries of the gold-bearing dirt.

The apex of the "V" was evidently the man's goal. Often he ran his eye along the converging sides and on up the hill, trying to divine the apex, the point where the gold-bearing dirt must cease. Here resided "Mr. Pocket"—for so the man familiarly addressed the imaginary point above him on the slope, crying out:

"Come down out o' that, Mr. Pocket! Be right smart an' agreeable, an' come down!"

"All right," he would add later, in a voice resigned to determination. "All right, Mr. Pocket. It's plain to me I got to come right up an' snatch you out bald-headed. An' I'll do it! I'll do it!" he would threaten still later.

Each pan he carried down to the water to wash, and as he went higher up the hill the pans grew richer, until he began to save the gold in an empty baking-powder can which he carried carelessly in his hip-pocket. So engrossed was he in his toil that he did not notice the long twilight of oncoming night. It was not until he tried vainly to see the gold colors in the bottom of the pan that he realized the passage of time. He straightened up abruptly. An expression of whimsical wonderment and awe overspread his face as he drawled:

"Gosh darn my buttons! if I didn't plumb forget dinner!"

He stumbled across the stream in the darkness and lighted his long-delayed fire. Flapjacks and bacon and warmed-over beans constituted his supper. Then he smoked a pipe by the smouldering coals, listening to the night noises and watching the moonlight stream through the canyon. After that he unrolled his bed, took off his heavy shoes, and pulled the blankets up to his chin. His face showed white in the moonlight, like the face of a corpse. But it was a corpse that knew its resurrection, for the man rose suddenly on one elbow and gazed across at his hillside.

"Good night, Mr. Pocket," he called sleepily. "Good night."

He slept through the early gray of morning until the direct rays of the sun smote his closed eyelids, when he awoke with a start and looked about him until he had established the continuity of his existence and identified his present self with the days previously lived.

To dress, he had merely to buckle on his shoes. He glanced at his fireplace and at his hillside, wavered, but fought down the temptation and started the fire.

"Keep yer shirt on, Bill; keep yer shirt on," he admonished himself. "What's the good of rushin'? No use in gettin' all het up an' sweaty. Mr. Pocket'll wait for you. He ain't a-runnin' away before you can get yer breakfast. Now, what you want, Bill, is something fresh in yer bill o' fare. So it's up to you to go an' get it."

He cut a short pole at the water's edge and drew from one of his pockets a bit of line and a draggled fly that had once been a royal coachman.

"Mebbe they'll bite in the early morning," he muttered, as he made his first cast into the pool. And a moment later he was gleefully crying: "What'd I tell you, eh? What'd I tell you?"

He had no reel, nor any inclination to waste time, and by main strength, and swiftly, he drew out of the water a flashing ten-inch trout. Three more, caught in rapid succession, furnished his breakfast. When he came to the stepping-stones on his way to his hillside, he was struck by a sudden thought, and paused.

"I'd just better take a hike down-stream a ways," he said. "There's no tellin' what cuss may be snoopin' around."

But he crossed over on the stones, and with a "I really oughter take that hike," the need of the precaution passed out of his mind and he fell to work.

At nightfall he straightened up. The small of his back was stiff from stooping toil, and as he put his hand behind him to soothe the protesting muscles, he said:

"Now what d'ye think of that, by damn? I clean forgot my dinner again! If I don't watch out, I'll sure be degeneratin' into a two-meal-a-day crank."

"Pockets is the damnedest things I ever see for makin' a man absent-minded," he communed that night, as he crawled into his blankets. Nor did he forget to call up the hillside, "Good night, Mr. Pocket! Good night!"

Rising with the sun, and snatching a hasty breakfast, he was early at work. A fever seemed to be growing in him, nor did the increasing richness of the test-pans allay this fever. There was a flush in his cheek other than that made by the heat of the sun, and he was oblivious to fatigue and the passage of time. When he filled a pan with dirt, he ran down the hill to wash it; nor could he forbear running up the hill again, panting and stumbling profanely, to refill the pan.

He was now a hundred yards from the water, and the inverted "V" was assuming definite proportions. The width of the pay-dirt steadily decreased, and the man extended in his mind's eye the sides of the "V" to their meeting-place far up the hill. This was his goal, the apex of the "V," and he panned many times to locate it.

"Just about two yards above that manzanita bush an' a yard to the right," he finally concluded.

Then the temptation seized him. "As plain as the nose on your face," he said, as he abandoned his laborious cross-cutting and climbed to the indicated apex. He filled a pan and carried it down the hill to wash. It contained no trace of gold. He dug deep, and he dug shallow, filling and washing a dozen pans, and was unrewarded even by the tiniest golden speck. He was enraged at having yielded to the temptation, and cursed himself blasphemously and pridelessly. Then he went down the hill and took up the cross-cutting.

"Slow an' certain, Bill; slow an' certain," he crooned. "Short-cuts to fortune ain't in your line, an' it's about time you know it. Get wise, Bill; get wise. Slow an' certain's the only hand you can play; so go to it, an' keep to it, too."

As the cross-cuts decreased, showing that the sides of the "V" were converging, the depth of the "V" increased. The gold-trace was dipping into the hill. It was only at thirty inches beneath the surface that he could get colors in his pan. The dirt he found at twenty-five inches from the surface, and at thirty-five inches, yielded barren pans. At the base of the "V," by the water's edge, he had found the gold colors at the grass roots. The higher he went up the hill, the deeper the gold dipped. To dig a hole three feet deep in order to get one test-pan was a task of no mean magnitude; while between the man and the apex intervened an untold number of such holes to be dug. "An' there's no tellin' how much deeper it'll pitch," he sighed, in a moment's pause, while his fingers soothed his aching back.

Feverish with desire, with aching back and stiffening muscles, with pick and shovel gouging and mauling the soft brown earth, the man toiled up the hill. Before him was the smooth slope, spangled with flowers and made sweet with their breath. Behind him was devastation. It looked like some terrible eruption breaking out on the smooth skin of the hill. His slow progress was like that of a slug, befouling beauty with a monstrous trail.

Though the dipping gold-trace increased the man's work, he found consolation in the increasing richness of the pans. Twenty cents, thirty cents, fifty cents, sixty cents, were the values of the gold found in the pans, and at nightfall he washed his banner pan, which gave him a dollar's worth of gold-dust from a shovelful of dirt.

"I'll just bet it's my luck to have some inquisitive cuss come buttin' in here on my pasture," he mumbled sleepily that night as he pulled the blankets up to his chin.

Suddenly he sat upright. "Bill!" he called sharply. "Now, listen to me, Bill; d'ye hear! It's up to you, to-morrow mornin', to mosey round an' see what you can see. Understand? Tomorrow morning, an' don't you forget it!"

He yawned and glanced across at his side-hill. "Good night, Mr. Pocket," he called.

In the morning he stole a march on the sun, for he had finished breakfast when its first rays caught him, and he was climbing the wall of the canyon where it crumbled away and gave footing. From the outlook at the top he found himself in the midst of loneliness. As far as he could see, chain after chain of mountains heaved themselves into his vision. To the east his eyes, leaping the miles between range and range and between many ranges, brought up at last against the white-peaked Sierras—the main crest, where the backbone of the Western world reared itself against the sky. To the north and south he could see more distinctly the cross-systems that broke through the main trend of the sea of mountains. To the west the ranges fell away, one behind the other, diminishing and fading into the gentle foothills that, in turn, descended into the great valley which he could not see.

And in all that mighty sweep of earth he saw no sign of man nor of the handiwork of man—save only the torn bosom of the hillside at his feet. The man looked long and carefully. Once, far down his own canyon, he thought he saw in the air a faint hint of smoke. He looked again and decided that it was the purple haze of the hills made dark by a convolution of the canyon wall at its back.

"Hey, you, Mr. Pocket!" he called down into the canyon. "Stand out from under! I'm a-comin', Mr. Pocket! I'm a-comin'!"

The heavy brogans on the man's feet made him appear clumsy-footed, but he swung down from the giddy height as lightly and airily as a mountain goat. A rock, turning under his foot on the edge of the precipice, did not disconcert him. He seemed to know the precise time required for the turn to culminate in disaster, and in the meantime he utilized the false footing itself for the momentary earth-contact necessary to carry him on into safety. Where the earth sloped so steeply that it was impossible to stand for a second upright, the man did not hesitate. His foot pressed the impossible surface for but a fraction of the fatal second and gave him the bound that carried him onward. Again, where even the fraction of a second's footing was out of the question, he would swing his body past by a moment's hand-grip on a jutting knob of rock, a crevice, or a precariously rooted shrub. At last, with a wild leap and yell, he exchanged the face of the wall for an earth-slide and finished the descent in the midst of several tons of sliding earth and gravel.

His first pan of the morning washed out over two dollars in coarse gold. It was from the centre of the "V." To either side the diminution in the values of the pans was swift. His lines of cross-cutting holes were growing very short. The converging sides of the inverted "V" were only a few yards apart. Their meeting-point was only a few yards above him. But the pay-streak was dipping deeper and deeper into the earth. By early afternoon he was sinking the test-holes five feet before the pans could show the gold-trace.

For that matter, the gold-trace had become something more than a trace; it was a placer mine in itself, and the man resolved to come back after he had found the pocket and work over the ground. But the increasing richness of the pans began to worry him. By late afternoon the worth of the pans had grown to three and four dollars. The man scratched his head perplexedly and looked a few feet up the hill at the manzanita bush that marked approximately the apex of the "V." He nodded his head and said oracularly:

"It's one o' two things, Bill; one o' two things. Either Mr. Pocket's spilled himself all out an' down the hill, or else Mr. Pocket's that damned rich you maybe won't be able to carry him all away with you. And that'd be hell, wouldn't it, now?" He chuckled at contemplation of so pleasant a dilemma.

Nightfall found him by the edge of the stream, his eyes wrestling with the gathering darkness over the washing of a five-dollar pan.

"Wisht I had an electric light to go on working," he said.

He found sleep difficult that night. Many times he composed himself and closed his eyes for slumber to overtake him; but his blood pounded with too strong desire, and as many times his eyes opened and he murmured wearily, "Wisht it was sun-up."

Sleep came to him in the end, but his eyes were open with the first paling of the stars, and the gray of dawn caught him with breakfast finished and climbing the hillside in the direction of the secret abiding-place of Mr. Pocket.

The first cross-cut the man made, there was space for only three holes, so narrow had become the pay-streak and so close was he to the fountainhead of the golden stream he had been following for four days.

"Be ca'm, Bill; be ca'm," he admonished himself, as he broke ground for the final hole where the sides of the "V" had at last come together in a point.

"I've got the almighty cinch on you, Mr. Pocket, an' you can't lose me," he said many times as he sank the hole deeper and deeper.

Four feet, five feet, six feet, he dug his way down into the earth. The digging grew harder. His pick grated on broken rock. He examined the rock. "Rotten quartz," was his conclusion as, with the shovel, he cleared the bottom of the hole of loose dirt. He attacked the crumbling quartz with the pick, bursting the disintegrating rock asunder with every stroke.

He thrust his shovel into the loose mass. His eye caught a gleam of yellow. He dropped the shovel and squatted suddenly on his heels. As a farmer rubs the clinging earth from fresh-dug potatoes, so the man, a piece of rotten quartz held in both hands, rubbed the dirt away.

"Sufferin' Sardanopolis!" he cried. "Lumps an' chunks of it! Lumps an' chunks of it!"

It was only half rock he held in his hand. The other half was virgin gold. He dropped it into his pan and examined another piece. Little yellow was to be seen, but with his strong fingers he crumbled the rotten quartz away till both hands were filled with glowing yellow. He rubbed the dirt away from fragment after fragment, tossing them into the gold-pan. It was a treasure-hole. So much had the quartz rotted away that there was less of it than there was of gold. Now and again he found a piece to which no rock clung—a piece that was all gold. A chunk, where the pick had laid open the heart of the gold, glittered like a handful of yellow jewels, and he cocked his head at it and slowly turned it around and over to observe the rich play of the light upon it.

"Talk about yer Too Much Gold diggin's!" the man snorted contemptuously. "Why, this diggin' 'd make it look like thirty cents. This diggin' is All Gold. An' right here an' now I name this yere canyon 'All Gold Canyon,' b' gosh!"

Still squatting on his heels, he continued examining the fragments and tossing them into the pan. Suddenly there came to him a premonition of danger. It seemed a shadow had fallen upon him. But there was no shadow. His heart had given a great jump up into his throat and was choking him. Then his blood slowly chilled and he felt the sweat of his shirt cold against his flesh.

He did not spring up nor look around. He did not move. He was considering the nature of the premonition he had received, trying to locate the source of the mysterious force that had warned him, striving to sense the imperative presence of the unseen thing that threatened him. There is an aura of things hostile, made manifest by messengers too refined for the senses to know; and this aura he felt, but knew not how he felt it. His was the feeling as when a cloud passes over the sun. It seemed that between him and life had passed something dark and smothering and menacing; a gloom, as it were, that swallowed up life and made for death—his death.

Every force of his being impelled him to spring up and confront the unseen danger, but his soul dominated the panic, and he remained squatting on his heels, in his hands a chunk of gold. He did not dare to look around, but he knew by now that there was something behind him and above him. He made believe to be interested in the gold in his hand. He examined it critically, turned it over and over, and rubbed the dirt from it. And all the time he knew that something behind him was looking at the gold over his shoulder.

Still feigning interest in the chunk of gold in his hand, he listened intently and he heard the breathing of the thing behind him. His eyes searched the ground in front of him for a weapon, but they saw only the uprooted gold, worthless to him now in his extremity. There was his pick, a handy weapon on occasion; but this was not such an occasion. The man realized his predicament. He was in a narrow hole that was seven feet deep. His head did not come to the surface of the ground. He was in a trap.

He remained squatting on his heels. He was quite cool and collected; but his mind, considering every factor, showed him only his helplessness. He continued rubbing the dirt from the quartz fragments and throwing the gold into the pan. There was nothing else for him to do. Yet he knew that he would have to rise up, sooner or later, and face the danger that breathed at his back. The minutes passed, and with the passage of each minute he knew that by so much he was nearer the time when he must stand up, or else—and his wet shirt went cold against his flesh again at the thought— or else he might receive death as he stooped there over his treasure.

Still he squatted on his heels, rubbing dirt from gold and debating in just what manner he should rise up. He might rise up with a rush and claw his way out of the hole to meet whatever threatened on the even footing above ground. Or he might rise up slowly and carelessly, and feign casually to discover the thing that breathed at his back. His instinct and every fighting fibre of his body favored the mad, clawing rush to the surface. His intellect, and the craft thereof, favored the slow and cautious meeting with the thing that menaced and which he could not see. And while he debated, a loud, crashing noise burst on his ear. At the same instant he received a stunning blow on the left side of the back, and from the point of impact felt a rush of flame through his flesh. He sprang up in the air, but halfway to his feet collapsed. His body crumpled in like a leaf withered in sudden heat, and he came down, his chest across his pan of gold, his face in the dirt and rock, his legs tangled and twisted because of the restricted space at the bottom of the hole. His legs twitched convulsively several times. His body was shaken as with a mighty ague. There was a slow expansion of the lungs, accompanied by a deep sigh. Then the air was slowly, very slowly, exhaled, and his body as slowly flattened itself down into inertness.

Above, revolver in hand, a man was peering down over the edge of the hole. He peered for a long time at the prone and motionless body beneath him. After a while the stranger sat down on the edge of the hole so that he could see into it, and rested the revolver on his knee. Reaching his hand into a pocket, he drew out a wisp of brown paper. Into this he dropped a few crumbs of tobacco. The combination became a cigarette, brown and squat, with the ends turned in. Not once did he take his eyes from the body at the bottom of the hole. He lighted the cigarette and drew its smoke into his lungs with a caressing intake of the breath. He smoked slowly. Once the cigarette went out and he relighted it. And all the while he studied the body beneath him.

In the end he tossed the cigarette stub away and rose to his feet. He moved to the edge of the hole. Spanning it, a hand resting on each edge, and with the revolver still in the right hand, he muscled his body down into the hole. While his feet were yet a yard from the bottom he released his hands and dropped down.

At the instant his feet struck bottom he saw the pocket-miner's arm leap out, and his own legs knew a swift, jerking grip that over-threw him. In the nature of the jump his revolver-hand was above his head. Swiftly as the grip had flashed about his legs, just as swiftly he brought the revolver down. He was still in the air, his fall in pro-cess of completion, when he pulled the trigger. The explosion was deafening in the confined space. The smoke filled the hole so that he could see nothing. He struck the bottom on his back, and like a cat's the pocket-miner's body was on top of him. Even as the min-er's body passed on top, the stranger crooked in his right arm to fire; and even in that instant the miner, with a quick thrust of el-bow, struck his wrist. The muzzle was thrown up and the bullet thudded into the dirt of the side of the hole.

The next instant the stranger felt the miner's hand grip his wrist. The struggle was now for the revolver. Each man strove to turn it against the other's body. The smoke in the hole was clearing. The stranger, lying on his back, was beginning to see dimly. But sud-denly he was blinded by a handful of dirt deliberately flung into his eyes by his antagonist. In that moment of shock his grip on the re-volver was broken. In the next moment he felt a smashing darkness descend upon his brain, and in the midst of the darkness even the darkness ceased.

But the pocket-miner fired again and again, until the revolver was empty. Then he tossed it from him and, breathing heavily, sat down on the dead man's legs.

The miner was sobbing and struggling for breath. "Measly skunk!" he panted; "a-campin' on my trail an' lettin' me do the work, an' then shootin' me in the back!"

He was half crying from anger and exhaustion. He peered at the face of the dead man. It was sprinkled with loose dirt and gravel, and it was difficult to distinguish the features.

"Never laid eyes on him before," the miner concluded his scru-tiny. "Just a common an' ordinary thief, damn him! An' he shot me in the back! He shot me in the back!"

He opened his shirt and felt himself, front and back, on his left side.

"Went clean through, and no harm done!" he cried jubilantly. "I'll bet he aimed all right all right; but he drew the gun over when he pulled the trigger—the cuss! But I fixed 'm! Oh, I fixed 'm!"

His fingers were investigating the bullet-hole in his side, and a shade of regret passed over his face. "It's goin' to be stiffer'n hell," he said. "An' it's up to me to get mended an' get out o' here."

He crawled out of the hole and went down the hill to his camp. Half an hour later he returned, leading his pack-horse. His open shirt disclosed the rude bandages with which he had dressed his wound. He was slow and awkward with his left-hand movements, but that did not prevent his using the arm.

The bight of the pack-rope under the dead man's shoulders enabled him to heave the body out of the hole. Then he set to work gathering up his gold. He worked steadily for several hours, pausing often to rest his stiffening shoulder and to exclaim:

"He shot me in the back, the measly skunk! He shot me in the back!"

When his treasure was quite cleaned up and wrapped securely into a number of blanket-covered parcels, he made an estimate of its value.

"Four hundred pounds, or I'm a Hottentot," he concluded. "Say two hundred in quartz an' dirt—that leaves two hundred pounds of gold. Bill! Wake up! Two hundred pounds of gold! Forty thousand dollars! An' it's yourn—all yourn!"

He scratched his head delightedly and his fingers blundered into an unfamiliar groove. They quested along it for several inches. It was a crease through his scalp where the second bullet had ploughed.

He walked angrily over to the dead man.

"You would, would you?" he bullied. "You would, eh? Well, I fixed you good an' plenty, an' I'll give you decent burial, too. That's more'n you'd have done for me."

He dragged the body to the edge of the hole and toppled it in. It struck the bottom with a dull crash, on its side, the face twisted up to the light. The miner peered down at it.

"An' you shot me in the back!" he said accusingly.

With pick and shovel he filled the hole. Then he loaded the gold on his horse. It was too great a load for the animal, and when he gained his camp he transferred part of it to his saddle-horse. Even so, he was compelled to abandon a portion of his outfit—pick and shovel and gold-pan, extra food and cooking utensils, and divers odds and ends.

The sun was at the zenith when the man forced the horses at the screen of vines and creepers. To climb the huge boulders the animals were compelled to uprear and struggle blindly through the tangled mass of vegetation. Once the saddle-horse fell heavily and the man removed the pack to get the animal on its feet. After it started on its way again the man thrust his head out from among the leaves and peered up at the hillside.

"The measly skunk!" he said, and disappeared.

There was a ripping and tearing of vines and boughs. The trees surged back and forth, marking the passage of the animals through the midst of them. There was a clashing of steel-shod hoofs on stone, and now and again an oath or a sharp cry of command. Then the voice of the man was raised in song:—

"Tu'n around an' tu'n yo' face
Untoe them sweet hills of grace
   (D' pow'rs of sin yo' am scornin'!).
Look about an' look aroun',
Fling yo' sin-pack on d' groun'
   (Yo' will meet wid d' Lord in d' mornin'!)."

The song grew faint and fainter, and through the silence crept back the spirit of the place. The stream once more drowsed and whispered; the hum of the mountain bees rose sleepily. Down through the perfume-weighted air fluttered the snowy fluffs of the cottonwoods. The butterflies drifted in and out among the trees, and over all blazed the quiet sunshine. Only remained the hoof-marks in the meadow and the torn hillside to mark the boisterous trail of the life that had broken the peace of the place and passed on.

6.

A Raid on the
Oyster Pirates

Jack London was only fifteen years old when he decided that working long hours in an Oakland cannery for small wages was incompatible with the kind of life he had read and dreamed about. He hated his drab existence, so he joined the ranks of the oyster pirates, a group of thieves and ruffians who raided the private oyster beds in the shallows of San Francisco Bay by night for handsome profits in the ready markets of the day. But he soon found this life to be precarious at best, and was persuaded by Charley Le Grant, the namesake of one of the protagonists in the following story, to become a deputy on the law enforcement agency known as the Fish Patrol. Here was a different world in which London hoped to find life more dignified and perhaps safer.

Later, when asked about the authenticity of the stories contained in the collection Tales of the Fish Patrol, London declared that "A Raid on the Oyster Pirates" was almost literally a narrative of an actual raid. All except the ending, in which London the storyteller blends fact and fiction for dramatic effect.

Written during the early years of the century with a young audience in mind, the stories still provide colorful adventures for readers of all ages.

George and Carrie Sterling and Jack London aboard the *Phyllis* in San Francisco Bay, 1909.

A RAID ON THE
OYSTER PIRATES

OF THE FISH PATROLMEN UNDER WHOM WE SERVED AT various times, Charley Le Grant and I were agreed, I think, that Neil Partington was the best. He was neither dishonest nor cowardly; and while he demanded strict obedience when we were under his orders, at the same time our relations were those of easy comradeship, and he permitted us a freedom to which we were ordinarily unaccustomed, as the present story will show.

Neil's family lived in Oakland, which is on the Lower Bay, not more than six miles across the water from San Francisco. One day, while scouting among the Chinese shrimp-catchers of Point Pedro, he received word that his wife was very ill; and within the hour the *Reindeer* was bowling along for Oakland, with a stiff northwest breeze astern. We ran up the Oakland Estuary and came to anchor, and in the days that followed, while Neil was ashore, we tightened up the *Reindeer's* rigging, overhauled the ballast, scraped down, and put the sloop into thorough shape.

This done, time hung heavy on our hands. Neil's wife was dangerously ill, and the outlook was a week's lie-over, awaiting the crisis. Charley and I roamed the docks, wondering what we should do, and so came upon the oyster fleet lying at the Oakland City Wharf. In the main they were trim, natty boats, made for speed and bad weather, and we sat down on the stringer-piece of the dock to study them.

"A good catch, I guess," Charley said, pointing to the heaps of oysters, assorted in three sizes, which lay upon their decks.

Peddlers were backing their wagons to the edge of the wharf, and from the bargaining and chaffering that went on, I managed to learn the selling price of the oysters.

"That boat must have at least two hundred dollars' worth aboard," I calculated. "I wonder how long it took to get the load?"

"Three or four days," Charley answered. "Not bad wages for two men—twenty-five dollars a day apiece."

The boat we were discussing, the *Ghost*, lay directly beneath us.

Two men composed its crew. One was a squat, broad-shouldered fellow with remarkably long and gorilla-like arms, while the other was tall and well proportioned, with clear blue eyes and a mat of straight black hair. So unusual and striking was this combination of hair and eyes that Charley and I remained somewhat longer than we intended.

And it was well that we did. A stout, elderly man, with the dress and carriage of a successful merchant, came up and stood beside us, looking down upon the deck of the *Ghost*. He appeared angry, and the longer he looked the angrier he grew.

"Those are my oysters," he said at last. "I know they are my oysters. You raided my beds last night and robbed me of them."

The tall man and the short man on the *Ghost* looked up.

"Hello, Taft," the short man said, with insolent familiarity. (Among the bayfarers he had gained the nickname of "The Centipede" on account of his long arms.) "Hello, Taft," he repeated, with the same touch of insolence. "Wot 'r you growlin' about now?"

"Those are my oysters—that's what I said. You've stolen them from my beds."

"Yer mighty wise, ain't ye?" was the Centipede's sneering reply. "S'pose you can tell your oysters wherever you see 'em?"

"Now, in my experience," broke in the tall man, "oysters is oysters wherever you find 'em, an' they're pretty much alike all the Bay over, and the world over, too, for that matter. We're not wantin' to quarrel with you, Mr. Taft, but we jes' wish you wouldn't insinuate that them oysters is yours an' that we're thieves an' robbers till you can prove the goods."

"I know they're mine; I'd stake my life on it!" Mr. Taft snorted.

"Prove it," challenged the tall man, who we afterward learned was known as "The Porpoise" because of his wonderful swimming abilities.

Mr. Taft shrugged his shoulders helplessly. Of course he could not prove the oysters to be his, no matter how certain he might be.

"I'd give a thousand dollars to have you men behind the bars!" he cried. "I'll give fifty dollars a head for your arrest and conviction, all of you!"

A roar of laughter went up from the different boats, for the rest of the pirates had been listening to the discussion.

"There's more money in oysters," the Porpoise remarked dryly.

Mr. Taft turned impatiently on his heel and walked away. From out of the corner of his eye, Charley noted the way he went. Several minutes later, when he had disappeared around a corner, Charley rose lazily to his feet. I followed him, and we sauntered off in the opposite direction to that taken by Mr. Taft.

"Come on! Lively!" Charley whispered, when we passed from the view of the oyster fleet.

Our course was changed at once, and we dodged around corners and raced up and down side-streets till Mr. Taft's generous form loomed up ahead of us.

"I'm going to interview him about that reward," Charley explained, as we rapidly overhauled the oyster-bed owner. "Neil will be delayed here for a week, and you and I might as well be doing something in the meantime. What do you say?"

"Of course, of course," Mr. Taft said, when Charley had introduced himself and explained his errand. "Those thieves are robbing me of thousands of dollars every year, and I shall be glad to break them up at any price—yes, sir, at any price. As I said, I'll give fifty dollars a head, and call it cheap at that. They've robbed my beds, torn down my signs, terrorized my watchmen, and last year killed one of them. Couldn't prove it. All done in the blackness of night. All I had was a dead watchman and no evidence. The detectives could do nothing. Nobody has been able to do anything with those men. We have never succeeded in arresting one of them. So I say, Mr.—What did you say your name was?"

"Le Grant," Charley answered.

"So I say, Mr. Le Grant, I am deeply obliged to you for the assistance you offer. And I shall be glad, most glad, sir, to cooperate with you in every way. My watchmen and boats are at your disposal. Come and see me at the San Francisco offices any time, or telephone at my expense. And don't be afraid of spending money. I'll foot your expenses, whatever they are, so long as they are within reason. The situation is growing desperate, and something must be done to determine whether I or that band of ruffians own those oyster beds."

"Now we'll see Neil," Charley said, when he had seen Mr. Taft upon his train to San Francisco.

Not only did Neil Partington interpose no obstacle to our adventure, but he proved to be of the greatest assistance. Charley and I knew nothing of the oyster industry, while his head was an encyclopedia of facts concerning it. Also, within an hour or so, he was able to bring to us a Greek boy of seventeen or eighteen who knew thoroughly well the ins and outs of oyster piracy.

At this point I may as well explain that we of the fish patrol were free lances in a way. While Neil Partington, who was a patrolman proper, received a regular salary, Charley and I, being merely deputies, received only what we earned—that is to say, a certain percentage of the fines imposed on convicted violators of the fish laws. Also, any rewards that chanced our way were ours. We offered to share with Partington whatever we should get from Mr. Taft, but the patrolman would not hear of it. He was only too happy, he said, to do a good turn for us, who had done so many for him.

We held a long council of war, and mapped out the following line of action. Our faces were unfamiliar on the Lower Bay, but as the *Reindeer* was well known as a fish-patrol sloop, the Greek boy, whose name was Nicholas, and I were to sail some innocent-looking craft down to Asparagus Island and join the oyster pirates' fleet. Here, according to Nicholas's description of the beds and the manner of raiding, it was possible for us to catch the pirates in the act of stealing oysters, and at the same time to get them in our power. Charley was to be on the shore, with Mr. Taft's watchmen and a posse of constables, to help us at the right time.

"I know just the boat," Neil said, at the conclusion of the discussion, "a crazy old sloop that's lying over at Tiburon. You and Nicholas can go over by the ferry, charter it for a song, and sail direct for the beds."

"Good luck be with you, boys," he said at parting, two days later. "Remember, they are dangerous men, so be careful."

Nicholas and I succeeded in chartering the sloop very cheaply; and between laughs, while getting up sail, we agreed that she was even crazier and older than she had been described. She was a big, flat-bottomed, square-sterned craft, sloop-rigged, with a sprung mast, slack rigging, dilapidated sails, and rotten running-gear, clumsy to handle and uncertain in bringing about, and she smelled vilely of coal tar, with which strange stuff she had been smeared from stem to stern and from cabin-roof to centreboard. And to cap it all, *Coal Tar Maggie* was printed in great white letters the whole length of either side.

It was an uneventful though laughable run from Tiburon to Asparagus Island, where we arrived in the afternoon of the following day. The oyster pirates, a fleet of a dozen sloops, were lying at anchor on what was known as the "Deserted Beds." The *Coal Tar Maggie* came sloshing into their midst with a light breeze astern, and they crowded on deck to see us. Nicholas and I had caught the spirit of the crazy craft, and we handled her in most lubberly fashion.

"Wot is it?" someone called.

"Name it 'n' ye kin have it!" called another.

"I swan naow, ef it ain't the old Ark itself!" mimicked the Centipede from the deck of the *Ghost.*

"Hey! Ahoy there, clipper ship!" another wag shouted. "Wot's yer port?"

We took no notice of the joking, but acted, after the manner of greenhorns, as though the *Coal Tar Maggie* required our undivided attention. I rounded her well to windward of the *Ghost*, and Nicholas ran for'ard to drop the anchor. To all appearances it was a bungle, the way the chain tangled and kept the anchor from reaching the bottom. And to all appearances Nicholas and I were terribly excited as we strove to clear it. At any rate, we quite deceived the pirates, who took huge delight in our predicament.

But the chain remained tangled, and amid all kinds of mocking advice we drifted down upon and fouled the *Ghost*, whose bowsprit poked square through our mainsail and ripped a hole in it as big as a barn door. The Centipede and the Porpoise doubled up on the cabin in paroxysms of laughter, and left us to get clear as best we could. This, with much unseamanlike performance, we succeeded in doing, and likewise in clearing the anchor-chain, of which we let out about three hundred feet. With only ten feet of water under us, this would permit the *Coal Tar Maggie* to swing in a circle six hundred feet in diameter, in which circle she would be able to foul at least half the fleet.

The oyster pirates lay snugly together at short hawsers, the weather being fine, and they protested loudly at our ignorance in putting out such an unwarranted length of anchor-chain. And not only did they protest, for they made us heave it in again, all but thirty feet.

Having sufficiently impressed them with our general lubberliness, Nicholas and I went below to congratulate ourselves and to cook supper. Hardly had we finished the meal and washed the dishes, when a skiff ground against the *Coal Tar Maggie's* side, and heavy feet trampled on deck. Then the Centipede's brutal face appeared in the companionway, and he descended into the cabin, followed by the Porpoise. Before they could seat themselves on a bunk, another skiff came alongside, and another, and another, till the whole fleet was represented by the gathering in the cabin.

"Where'd you swipe the old tub?" asked a squat and hairy man, with cruel eyes and Mexican features.

"Didn't swipe it," Nicholas answered, meeting them on their own ground and encouraging the idea that we had stolen the *Coal Tar Maggie*. "And if we did, what of it?"

"Well, I don't admire your taste, that's all," sneered he of the Mexican features. "I'd rot on the beach first before I'd take a tub that couldn't get out of its own way."

"How were we to know till we tried her?" Nicholas asked, so innocently as to cause a laugh. "And how do you get the oysters?" he hurried on. "We want a load of them; that's what we came for, a load of oysters."

"What d'ye want 'em for?" demanded the Porpoise.

"Oh, to give away to our friends, of course," Nicholas retorted. "That's what you do with yours, I suppose."

This started another laugh, and as our visitors grew more genial we could see that they had not the slightest suspicion of our identity or purpose.

"Didn't I see you on the dock in Oakland the other day?" the Centipede asked suddenly of me.

"Yep," I answered boldly, taking the bull by the horns. "I was watching you fellows and figuring out whether we'd go oystering or not. It's a pretty good business, I calculate, and so we're going in for it. That is," I hastened to add, "if you fellows don't mind."

"I'll tell you one thing, which ain't two things," he replied, "and that is you'll have to hump yerself an' get a better boat. We won't stand to be disgraced by any such box as this. Understand?"

"Sure," I said. "Soon as we sell some oysters we'll outfit in style."

"And if you show yerself square an' the right sort," he went on, "why, you kin run with us. But if you don't" (here his voice became stern and menacing), "why, it'll be the sickest day of yer life. Understand?"

"Sure," I said.

After that and more warning and advice of similar nature, the conversation became general, and we learned that the beds were to be raided that very night. As they got into their boats, after an hour's stay, we were invited to join them in the raid with the assurance of "the more the merrier."

"Did you notice that short, Mexican-looking chap?" Nicholas asked, when they had departed to their various sloops. "He's Barchi, of the Sporting Life Gang, and the fellow that came with him is Skilling. They're both out now on five thousand dollars' bail."

I had heard of the Sporting Life Gang before, a crowd of hoodlums and criminals that terrorized the lower quarters of Oakland, and two-thirds of which were usually to be found in state's prison for crimes that ranged from perjury and ballot-box stuffing to murder.

"They are not regular oyster pirates," Nicholas continued. "They've just come down for the lark and to make a few dollars. But we'll have to watch out for them."

We sat in the cockpit and discussed the details of our plan till eleven o'clock had passed, when we heard the rattle of an oar in a boat from the direction of the *Ghost*. We hauled up our own skiff, tossed in a few sacks, and rowed over. There we found all the skiffs assembling, it being the intention to raid the beds in a body.

To my surprise, I found barely a foot of water where we had dropped anchor in ten feet. It was the big June run-out of the full moon, and as the ebb had yet an hour and a half to run, I knew that our anchorage would be dry ground before slack water.

Mr. Taft's beds were three miles away, and for a long time we rowed silently in the wake of the other boats, once in a while grounding and our oar blades constantly striking bottom. At last we came upon soft mud covered with not more than two inches of water—not enough to float the boats. But the pirates at once were over the side, and by pushing and pulling on the flat-bottomed skiffs, we moved steadily along.

The full moon was partly obscured by high-flying clouds, but the pirates went their way with the familiarity born of long practice. After half a mile of the mud, we came upon a deep channel, up which we rowed, with dead oyster shoals looming high and dry on either side. At last we reached the picking grounds. Two men, on one of the shoals, hailed us and warned us off. But the Centipede, the Porpoise, Barchi, and Skilling took the lead, and followed by the rest of us, at least thirty men in half as many boats, rowed right up to the watchmen.

"You'd better slide outa this here," Barchi said threateningly, "or we'll fill you so full of holes you wouldn't float in molasses."

The watchmen wisely retreated before so overwhelming a force, and rowed their boat along the channel toward where the shore should be. Besides, it was in the plan for them to retreat.

We hauled the noses of the boats up on the shore side of a big shoal, and all hands, with sacks, spread out and began picking. Every now and again the clouds thinned before the face of the moon, and we could see the big oysters quite distinctly. In almost no time sacks were filled and carried back to the boats, where fresh ones were obtained. Nicholas and I returned often and anxiously to the boats with our little loads, but always found some one of the pirates coming or going.

"Never mind," he said; "no hurry. As they pick farther and farther away, it will take too long to carry to the boats. Then they'll stand the full sacks on end and pick them up when the tide comes in and the skiffs will float to them."

Fully half an hour went by, and the tide had begun to flood, when this came to pass. Leaving the pirates at their work, we stole back to the boats. One by one, and noiselessly, we shoved them off and made them fast in an awkward flotilla. Just as we were shoving off the last skiff, our own, one of the men came upon us. It was Barchi. His quick eye took in the situation at a glance, and he sprang for us; but we went clear with a mighty shove, and he was left floundering in the water over his head. As soon as he got back to the shoal he raised his voice and gave the alarm.

We rowed with all our strength, but it was slow going with so many boats in tow. A pistol cracked from the shoal, a second, and a third; then a regular fusillade began. The bullets spat and spat all about us; but thick clouds had covered the moon, and in the dim darkness it was no more than random firing. It was only by chance that we could be hit.

"Wish we had a little steam launch," I panted.

"I'd just as soon the moon stayed hidden," Nicholas panted back.

It was slow work, but every stroke carried us farther away from the shoal and nearer the shore, till at last the shooting died down, and when the moon did come out we were too far away to be in danger. Not long afterward we answered a shoreward hail, and two Whitehall boats, each pulled by three pairs of oars, darted up to us. Charley's welcome face bent over to us, and he gripped us by the hands while he cried, "Oh, you joys! You joys! Both of you!"

When the flotilla had been landed, Nicholas and I and a watchman rowed out in one of the Whitehalls, with Charley in the stern-sheets. Two other Whitehalls followed us, and as the moon now shone brightly, we easily made out the oyster pirates on their lonely shoal. As we drew closer, they fired a rattling volley from their revolvers, and we promptly retreated beyond range.

"Lot of time," Charley said. "The flood is setting in fast, and by the time it's up to their necks there won't be any fight left in them."

So we lay on our oars and waited for the tide to do its work. This was the predicament of the pirates: because of the big run-out, the tide was now rushing back like a mill-race, and it was impossible for the strongest swimmer in the world to make against it the three miles to the sloops. Between the pirates and the shore were we, precluding escape in that direction. On the other hand, the water was rising rapidly over the shoals, and it was only a question of a few hours when it would be over their heads.

It was beautifully calm, and in the brilliant white moonlight we watched them through our night glasses and told Charley of the voyage of the *Coal Tar Maggie*. One o'clock came, and two o'clock, and the pirates were clustering on the highest shoal, waist-deep in water.

"Now this illustrates the value of imagination," Charley was saying. "Taft has been trying for years to get them, but he went at it with bull strength and failed. Now we used our heads . . ."

Just then I heard a scarcely audible gurgle of water, and holding up my hand for silence, I turned and pointed to a ripple slowly widening out in a growing circle. It was not more than fifty feet from us. We kept perfectly quiet and waited. After a minute the water broke six feet away, and a black head and white shoulder showed in the moonlight. With a snort of surprise and of suddenly expelled breath, the head and shoulder went down.

We pulled ahead several strokes and drifted with the current. Four pairs of eyes searched the surface of the water, but never another ripple showed, and never another glimpse did we catch of the black head and white shoulder.

"It's the Porpoise," Nicholas said. "It would take broad daylight for us to catch him."

At a quarter to three the pirates gave their first sign of weakening. We heard cries for help, in the unmistakable voice of the Centipede, and this time, on rowing closer, we were not fired upon. The Centipede was in a truly perilous plight. Only the heads and shoulders of his fellow-marauders showed above the water as they braced themselves against the current, while his feet were off the bottom and they were supporting him.

"Now, lads," Charley said briskly, "we have got you, and you can't get away. If you cut up rough, we'll have to leave you alone and the water will finish you. But if you're good, we'll take you aboard, one man at a time, and you'll all be saved. What do you say?"

"Ay," they chorused hoarsely between their chattering teeth.

"Then one man at a time, and the short men first."

The Centipede was the first to be pulled aboard, and he came willingly, though he objected when the constable put the handcuffs on him. Barchi was next hauled in, quite meek and resigned from his soaking. When we had ten in our boat we drew back, and the second Whitehall was loaded. The third Whitehall received nine prisoners only—a catch of twenty-nine in all.

"You didn't get the Porpoise," the Centipede said exultantly, as though his escape materially diminished our success.

Charley laughed. "But we saw him just the same, a-snorting for shore like a puffing pig."

It was a mild and shivering band of pirates that we marched up the beach to the oyster house. In answer to Charley's knock, the door was flung open, and a pleasant wave of warm air rushed out upon us.

"You can dry your clothes here, lads, and get some hot coffee," Charley announced, as they filed in.

And there, sitting ruefully by the fire, with a steaming mug in his hand, was the Porpoise. With one accord Nicholas and I looked at Charley. He laughed gleefully.

"That comes of imagination," he said. "When you see a thing, you've got to see it all around, or what's the good of seeing it at all? I saw the beach, so I left a couple of constables behind to keep an eye on it. That's all."

7.

Demetrios Contos

In reply to readers who wanted to know more about the source material for Jack London's "Fish Patrol" stories, the author was more than happy to explain. In March 1903, in a letter to an editor of the Youth's Companion, he wrote, "I have written of the years 1891 and 1892 in San Francisco Bay and up the rivers. The fishermen were then a wild crowd, as they still are a wild crowd but the oyster pirates are gone. . . . There is not so much shooting, etc. going on now among the Greeks and Italians as formerly, and they have been pretty well brought under the heel of the law."

London gathered material for these stories from his own experiences on San Francisco Bay with an array of characters with nicknames such as Spider Healy, Whiskey Bob, Scratch Nelson, Nicky the Greek, and French Frank. According to London, the story that follows "is a fiction which exceeds the truth. For in point of fact, Demetrios Contos would have left me to drown had the story actually occurred."

Fortunately for family, friends, and posterity, London was spared such a fate. And it is enlightening to know that some of the action within the story actually took place during his exploits on the Bay waters. "Pride in a fast boat," he said, "and the flaunting of the Fish Patrol," were a part of a way of life he experienced firsthand and wrote about.

French Frank and Jack London—more than likely reminiscing about their sailing and oyster-pirating days in the early 1890s.

DEMETRIOS CONTOS

IT MUST NOT BE THOUGHT, FROM WHAT I HAVE TOLD OF THE Greek fishermen, that they were altogether bad. Far from it. But they were rough men, gathered together in isolated communities and fighting with the elements for a livelihood. They lived far away from the law and its workings, did not understand it, and thought it tyranny. Especially did the fish laws seem tyrannical. And because of this, they looked upon the men of the fish patrol as their natural enemies.

We menaced their lives, or their living, which is the same thing, in many ways. We confiscated illegal traps and nets, the materials of which had cost them considerable sums and the making of which required weeks of labor. We prevented them from catching fish at many times and seasons, which was equivalent to preventing them from making as good a living as they might have made had we not been in existence. And when we captured them, they were brought into the courts of law, where heavy cash fines were collected from them. As a result, they hated us vindictively. As the dog is the natural enemy of the cat, the snake of man, so were we of the fish patrol the natural enemies of the fishermen.

But it is to show that they could act generously as well as hate bitterly that this story of Demetrios Contos is told. Demetrios Contos lived in Vallejo. Next to Big Alec, he was the largest, bravest, and most influential man among the Greeks. He had given us no trouble, and I doubt if he would ever have clashed with us had he not invested in a new salmon boat. This boat was the cause of all the trouble. He had had it built upon his own model, in which the lines of the general salmon boat were somewhat modified.

To his high elation he found his new boat very fast—in fact, faster than any other boat on the bay or rivers. Forthwith he grew proud and boastful: and, our raid with the *Mary Rebecca* on the Sunday salmon fishers having wrought fear in their hearts, he sent a challenge up to Benicia. One of the local fishermen conveyed it to us; it was to the effect that Demetrios Contos would sail up from Vallejo on the following Sunday, and in the plain sight of Benicia set his net and catch salmon, and that Charley Le Grant, patrolman, might come and get him if he could. Of course Charley and I had heard nothing of the new boat. Our own boat was pretty fast, and we were not afraid to have a brush with any other that happened along.

Sunday came. The challenge had been bruited abroad, and the fishermen and seafaring folk of Benicia turned out to a man, crowding Steamboat Wharf till it looked like the grand stand at a football match. Charley and I had been skeptical, but the fact of the crowd convinced us that there was something in Demetrios Contos's dare.

In the afternoon, when the sea-breeze had picked up in strength, his sail hove into view as he bowled along before the wind. He tacked a score of feet from the wharf, waved his hand theatrically, like a knight about to enter the lists, received a hearty cheer in return, and stood away into the Straits for a couple of hundred yards. Then he lowered sail, and, drifting the boat sidewise by means of the wind, proceeded to set his net. He did not set much of it, possibly fifty feet; yet Charley and I were thunderstruck at the man's effrontery. We did not know at the time, but we learned afterward, that the net he used was old and worthless. It *could* catch fish, true; but a catch of any size would have torn it to pieces.

Charley shook his head and said:

"I confess, it puzzles me. What if he has out only fifty feet? He could never get it in if we once started for him. And why does he come here anyway, flaunting his law-breaking in our faces? Right in our home town, too."

Charley's voice took on an aggrieved tone, and he continued for some minutes to inveigh against the brazenness of Demetrios Contos.

In the meantime, the man in question was lolling in the stern of his boat and watching the net floats. When a large fish is meshed in a gill-net, the floats by their agitation advertise the fact. And they evidently advertised it to Demetrios, for he pulled in about a dozen feet of net, and held aloft for a moment, before he flung it into the bottom of the boat, a big, glistening salmon. It was greeted by the audience on the wharf with round after round of cheers. This was more than Charley could stand.

"Come on, lad," he called to me; and we lost no time jumping into our salmon boat and getting up sail.

The crowd shouted warning to Demetrios, and as we darted out from the wharf we saw him slash his worthless net clear with a long knife. His sail was all ready to go up, and a moment later it fluttered in the sunshine. He ran aft, drew in the sheet, and filled on the long tack toward the Contra Costa Hills.

By this time we were not more than thirty feet astern. Charley was jubilant. He knew our boat was fast, and he knew, further, that in fine sailing few men were his equals. He was confident that we should surely catch Demetrios, and I shared his confidence. But somehow we did not seem to gain.

It was a pretty sailing breeze. We were gliding sleekly through the water, but Demetrios was slowly sliding away from us. And not only was he going faster, but he was eating into the wind a fraction of a point closer than we. This was sharply impressed upon us when he went about under the Contra Costa Hills and passed us on the other tack fully one hundred feet dead to windward.

"Whew!" Charley exclaimed. "Either that boat is a daisy, or we've got a five-gallon coal-oil can fast to our keel!"

It certainly looked it one way or the other. And by the time Demetrios made the Sonoma Hills, on the other side of the Straits, we were so hopelessly outdistanced that Charley told me to slack off the sheet, and we squared away for Benicia. The fishermen on Steamboat Wharf showered us with ridicule when we returned and tied up. Charley and I got out and walked away, feeling rather sheepish, for it is a sore stroke to one's pride when he thinks he has a good boat and knows how to sail it, and another man comes along and beats him.

Charley mooned over it for a couple of days; then word was brought to us, as before, that on the next Sunday Demetrios Contos would repeat his performance. Charley roused himself. He had our boat out of the water, cleaned and repainted its bottom, made a trifling alteration about the centre-board, overhauled the running gear, and sat up nearly all of Saturday night sewing on a new and much larger sail. So large did he make it, in fact, that additional ballast was imperative, and we stowed away nearly five hundred extra pounds of old railroad iron in the bottom of the boat.

Sunday came, and with it came Demetrios Contos, to break the law defiantly in open day. Again we had the afternoon sea-breeze, and again Demetrios cut loose some forty or more feet of his rotten net, and got up sail and under way under our very noses. But he had anticipated Charley's move, and his own sail peaked higher than ever, while a whole extra cloth had been added to the after leech.

It was nip and tuck across to the Contra Costa Hills, neither of us seeming to gain or to lose. But by the time we had made the return tack to the Sonoma Hills, we could see that, while we footed it at about equal speed, Demetrios had eaten into the wind the least bit more than we. Yet Charley was sailing our boat as finely and delicately as it was possible to sail it, and getting more out of it than he ever had before.

Of course, he could have drawn his revolver and fired at Demetrios; but we had long since found it contrary to our natures to shoot at a fleeing man guilty of only a petty offence. Also a sort of tacit agreement seemed to have been reached between the patrolmen and the fishermen. If we did not shoot while they ran away, they, in turn, did not fight if we once laid hands on them. Thus Demetrios Contos ran away from us, and we did no more than try our best to overtake him; and, in turn, if our boat proved faster than his, or was sailed better, he would, we knew, make no resistance when we caught up with him.

With our large sails and the healthy breeze romping up the Carquinez Straits, we found that our sailing was what is called "ticklish." We had to be constantly on the alert to avoid a capsize, and while Charley steered I held the main-sheet in my hand with but a single turn round a pin, ready to let go at any moment. Demetrios, we could see, sailing his boat alone, had his hands full.

But it was a vain undertaking for us to attempt to catch him. Out of his inner consciousness he had evolved a boat that was better than ours. And though Charley sailed fully as well, if not the least bit better, the boat he sailed was not so good as the Greek's.

"Slack away the sheet," Charley commanded; and as our boat fell off before the wind, Demetrios's mocking laugh floated down to us.

Charley shook his head, saying, "It's no use. Demetrios has the better boat. If he tries his performance again, we must meet it with some new scheme."

This time it was my imagination that came to the rescue.

"What's the matter," I suggested, on the Wednesday following, "with my chasing Demetrios in the boat next Sunday, while you wait for him on the wharf at Vallejo when he arrives?"

Charley considered it a moment and slapped his knee.

"A good idea! You're beginning to use that head of yours. A credit to your teacher, I must say."

"But you mustn't chase him too far," he went on, the next moment, "or he'll head out into San Pablo Bay instead of running home to Vallejo, and there I'll be, standing lonely on the wharf and waiting in vain for him to arrive."

On Thursday Charley registered an objection to my plan.

"Everybody'll know I've gone to Vallejo, and you can depend upon it that Demetrios will know, too. I'm afraid we'll have to give up the idea."

This objection was only too valid, and for the rest of the day I struggled under my disappointment. But that night a new way seemed to open to me, and in my eagerness I awoke Charley from a sound sleep.

"Well," he grunted, "what's the matter? House afire?"

"No," I replied, "but my head is. Listen to this. On Sunday you and I will be around Benicia up to the very moment Demetrios's sail heaves into sight. This will lull everybody's suspicions. Then, when Demetrios's sail does heave in sight, do you stroll leisurely away and up-town. All the fishermen will think you're beaten and that you know you're beaten."

"So far, so good," Charley commented, while I paused to catch breath.

"And very good indeed," I continued proudly. "You stroll carelessly up-town, but when you're once out of sight you leg it for all you're worth for Dan Maloney's. Take the little mare of his, and strike out on the county road for Vallejo. The road's in fine condition, and you can make it in quicker time than Demetrios can beat all the way down against the wind."

"And I'll arrange right away for the mare, first thing in the morning," Charley said, accepting the modified plan without hesitation.

"But, I say," he said, a little later, this time waking *me* out of a sound sleep.

I could hear him chuckling in the dark.

"I say, lad, isn't it rather a novelty for the fish patrol to be taking to horseback?"

"Imagination," I answered. "It's what you're always preaching— 'keep thinking one thought ahead of the other fellow, and you're bound to win out.' "

"He! he!" he chuckled. "And if one thought ahead, including a mare, doesn't take the other fellow's breath away this time, I'm not your humble servant, Charley Le Grant."

"But can you manage the boat alone?" he asked, on Friday. "Remember, we've a ripping big sail on her."

I argued my proficiency so well that he did not refer to the matter again till Saturday, when he suggested removing one whole cloth from the after leech. I guess it was the disappointment written on my face that made him desist; for I, also, had a pride in my boat-sailing abilities, and I was almost wild to get out alone with the big sail and go tearing down the Carquinez Straits in the wake of the flying Greek.

As usual, Sunday and Demetrios Contos arrived together. It had become the regular thing for the fishermen to assemble on Steamboat Wharf to greet his arrival and to laugh at our discomfiture. He lowered sail a couple of hundred yards out and set his customary fifty feet of rotten net.

"I suppose this nonsense will keep up as long as his old net holds out," Charley grumbled, with intention, in the hearing of several of the Greeks.

"Den I give-a heem my old-a net-a," one of them spoke up, promptly and maliciously.

"I don't care," Charley answered. "I've got some old net myself he can have—if he'll come around and ask for it."

They all laughed at this, for they could afford to be sweet-tempered with a man so badly outwitted as Charley was.

"Well, so long, lad," Charley called to me a moment later. "I think I'll go up-town to Maloney's."

"Let me take the boat out?" I asked.

"If you want to," was his answer, as he turned on his heel and walked slowly away.

Demetrios pulled two large salmon out of his net, and I jumped into the boat. The fishermen crowded around in a spirit of fun, and when I started to get up sail overwhelmed me with all sorts of jocular advice. They even offered extravagant bets to one another that I would surely catch Demetrios, and two of them, styling themselves the committee of judges, gravely asked permission to come along with me to see how I did it.

But I was in no hurry. I waited to give Charley all the time I could, and I pretended dissatisfaction with the stretch of the sail and slightly shifted the small tackle by which the huge sprit forces up the peak. It was not until I was sure that Charley had reached Dan Maloney's and was on the little mare's back, that I cast off from the wharf and gave the big sail to the wind. A stout puff filled it and suddenly pressed the lee gunwale down till a couple of buckets of water came inboard. A little thing like this will happen to the best small-boat sailors, and yet, though I instantly let go the sheet and righted, I was cheered sarcastically, as though I had been guilty of a very awkward blunder.

When Demetrios saw only one person in the fish patrol boat, and that one a boy, he proceeded to play with me. Making a short tack out, with me not thirty feet behind, he returned, with his sheet a little free, to Steamboat Wharf. And there he made short tacks, and turned and twisted and ducked around, to the great delight of his sympathetic audience. I was right behind him all the time, and I dared to do whatever he did, even when he squared away before the wind and jibed his big sail over—a most dangerous trick with such a sail in such a wind.

He depended upon the brisk sea-breeze and the strong ebb tide, which together kicked up a nasty sea, to bring me to grief. But I was on my mettle, and never in all my life did I sail a boat better than on that day. I was keyed up to concert pitch, my brain was working smoothly and quickly, my hands never fumbled once, and it seemed that I almost divined the thousand little things which a small-boat sailor must be taking into consideration every second.

It was Demetrios who came to grief instead. Something went wrong with his centre-board, so that it jammed in the case and would not go all the way down. In a moment's breathing space which he had gained from me by a clever trick, I saw him working impatiently with the centre-board, trying to force it down. I gave him little time, and he was compelled quickly to return to the tiller and sheet.

The centre-board made him anxious. He gave over playing with me, and started on the long beat to Vallejo. To my joy, on the first long tack across, I found that I could eat into the wind just a little bit closer than he. Here was where another man in the boat would have been of value to him; for, with me but a few feet astern, he did not dare let go the tiller and run amidships to try to force down the centre-board.

Unable to hang on as close in the eye of the wind as formerly, he proceeded to slack his sheet a trifle and to ease off a bit, in order to outfoot me. This I permitted him to do till I had worked to windward, when I bore down upon him. As I drew close, he feinted at coming about. This led me to shoot into the wind to forestall him. But it was only a feint, cleverly executed, and he held back to his course while I hurried to make up lost ground.

He was undeniably smarter than I when it came to maneuvering. Time after time I all but had him, and each time he tricked me and escaped. Besides, the wind was freshening constantly, and each of us had his hands full to avoid capsizing. As for my boat, it could not have been kept afloat but for the extra ballast. I sat cocked over the weather gunwale, tiller in one hand and sheet in the other; and the sheet, with a single turn around a pin, I was very often forced to let go in the severer puffs. This allowed the sail to spill the wind, which was equivalent to taking off so much driving power, and of course I lost ground. My consolation was that Demetrios was as often compelled to do the same thing.

The strong ebb-tide, racing down the Straits in the teeth of the wind, caused an unusually heavy and spiteful sea, which dashed aboard continually. I was dripping wet, and even the sail was wet half-way up the after leech. Once I did succeed in outmaneuvering Demetrios, so that my bow bumped into him amidships. Here was where I should have had another man. Before I could run forward and leap aboard, he shoved the boats apart with an oar, laughing mockingly in my face as he did so.

We were now at the mouth of the Straits, in a bad stretch of water. Here the Vallejo Straits and the Carquinez Straits rushed directly at each other. Through the first flowed all the water of Napa River and the great tide-lands; through the second flowed all the water of Suisun Bay and the Sacramento and San Joaquin rivers. And where such immense bodies of water, flowing swiftly, clashed together, a terrible tide-rip was produced. To make it worse, the wind howled up San Pablo Bay for fifteen miles and drove in a tremendous sea upon the tide-rip.

Conflicting currents tore about in all directions, colliding, forming whirlpools, sucks, and boils, and shooting up spitefully into hollow waves which fell aboard as often from leeward as from windward. And through it all, confused, driven into a madness of motion, thundered the great smoking seas from San Pablo Bay.

I was as wildly excited as the water. The boat was behaving splendidly, leaping and lurching through the welter like a race-horse. I could hardly contain myself with the joy of it. The huge sail, the howling wind, the driving seas, the plunging boat—I, a pygmy, a mere speck in the midst of it, was mastering the elemental strife, flying through it and over it, triumphant and victorious.

And just then, as I roared along like a conquering hero, the boat received a frightful smash and came instantly to a dead stop. I was flung forward and into the bottom. As I sprang up I caught a fleeting glimpse of a greenish, barnacle-covered object, and knew it at once for what it was, that terror of navigation, a sunken pile. No man may guard against such a thing. Water-logged and floating just beneath the surface, it was impossible to sight it in the troubled water in time to escape.

The whole bow of the boat must have been crushed in, for in a few seconds the boat was half full. Then a couple of seas filled it, and it sank straight down, dragged to bottom by the heavy ballast. So quickly did it all happen that I was entangled in the sail and drawn under. When I fought my way to the surface, suffocating, my lungs almost bursting, I could see nothing of the oars. They must have been swept away by the chaotic currents. I saw Demetrios Contos looking back from his boat, and heard the vindictive and mocking tones of his voice as he shouted exultantly. He held steadily on his course, leaving me to perish.

There was nothing to do but to swim for it, which, in that wild confusion, was at the best a matter of but a few moments. Holding my breath and working with my hands, I managed to get off my heavy sea-boots and my jacket. Yet there was very little breath I could catch to hold, and I swiftly discovered that it was not so much a matter of swimming as of breathing.

I was beaten and buffeted, smashed under by the great San Pablo whitecaps, and strangled by the hollow tide-rip waves which flung themselves into my eyes, nose, and mouth. Then the strange sucks would grip my legs and drag me under, to spout me up in some fierce boiling, where, even as I tried to catch my breath, a great whitecap would crash down upon my head.

It was impossible to survive any length of time. I was breathing more water than air, and drowning all the time. My senses began to leave me, my head to whirl around. I struggled on, spasmodically, instinctively, and was barely half conscious when I felt myself caught by the shoulders and hauled over the gunwale of a boat.

For some time I lay across a seat where I had been flung, face downward, and with the water running out of my mouth. After a while, still weak and faint, I turned around to see who was my rescuer. And there, in the stern, sheet in one hand and tiller in the other, grinning and nodding good-naturedly, sat Demetrios Contos. He had intended to leave me to drown—he said so afterward—but his better self had fought the battle, conquered, and sent him back to me.

"You all-a right?" he asked.

I managed to shape a "yes" on my lips, though I could not yet speak.

"You sail-a de boat verr-a good-a," he said. "So good-a as a man."

A compliment from Demetrios Contos was a compliment indeed, and I keenly appreciated it, though I could only nod my head in acknowledgment.

We held no more conversation, for I was busy recovering and he was busy with the boat. He ran in to the wharf at Vallejo, made the boat fast, and helped me out. Then it was, as we both stood on the wharf, that Charley stepped out from behind a net-rack and put his hand on Demetrios Contos's arm.

"He saved my life, Charley," I protested; "and I don't think he ought to be arrested."

A puzzled expression came into Charley's face, which cleared immediately after, in a way it had when he made up his mind.

"I can't help it, lad," he said kindly. "I can't go back on my duty, and it's plain duty to arrest him. To-day is Sunday; there are two salmon in his boat which he caught to-day. What else can I do?"

"But he saved my life," I persisted, unable to make any other argument.

Demetrios Contos's face went black with rage when he learned Charley's judgment. He had a sense of being unfairly treated. The better part of his nature had triumphed, he had performed a generous act and saved a helpless enemy, and in return the enemy was taking him to jail.

Charley and I were out of sorts with each other when we went back to Benicia. I stood for the spirit of the law and not the letter; but by the letter Charley made his stand. As far as he could see, there was nothing else for him to do. The law said distinctly that no salmon should be caught on Sunday. He was a patrolman, and it was his duty to enforce that law. That was all there was to it. He had done his duty, and his conscience was clear. Nevertheless, the whole thing seemed unjust to me, and I felt very sorry for Demetrios Contos.

Two days later we went down to Vallejo to the trial. I had to go along as a witness, and it was the most hateful task that I ever performed in my life when I testified on the witness stand to seeing Demetrios catch the two salmon Charley had captured him with.

Demetrios had engaged a lawyer, but his case was hopeless. The jury was out only fifteen minutes, and returned a verdict of guilty. The judge sentenced Demetrios to pay a fine of one hundred dollars or go to jail for fifty days.

Charley stepped up to the clerk of the court. "I want to pay that fine," he said, at the same time placing five twenty-dollar gold pieces on the desk. "It—it was the only way out of it, lad," he stammered, turning to me.

The moisture rushed into my eyes as I seized his hand. "I want to pay—" I began.

"To pay your half?" he interrupted. "I certainly shall expect you to pay it."

In the meantime Demetrios had been informed by his lawyer that his fee likewise had been paid by Charley.

Demetrios came over to shake Charley's hand, and all his warm Southern blood flamed in his face. Then, not to be outdone in generosity, he insisted on paying his fine and lawyer's fee himself, and flew half-way into a passion because Charley refused to let him.

More than anything else we ever did, I think, this action of Charley's impressed upon the fishermen the deeper significance of the law. Also Charley was raised high in their esteem, while I came in for a little share of praise as a boy who knew how to sail a boat. Demetrios Contos not only never broke the law again, but he became a very good friend of ours, and on more than one occasion he ran up to Benicia to have a gossip with us.

8.

Small-Boat Sailing

"Once a sailor, always a sailor," exclaims Jack London in this sprightly commentary on the art of sailing a small boat. At times he ventured out upon the open seas in larger vessels, but he makes clear that his own love affair with wind, wave, and sail began in a sloop on the varied and unpredictable waterways of San Francisco Bay.

No one, of course, was more aware of his genuine fondness for sailing than his wife, Charmian. He was "most blissfully content," she said, when he was in control of his own small craft. "Dawn or twilight, he loved the way of a boat upon the sea."

While still in his early teens, London had fairly well mastered the intricacies of handling a sloop—from the calm waters among the tules at the mouth of the Napa River to the treacherous heavy tides that rush through Carquinez Straits. At times he roamed down to the little port of Alviso in the South Bay, up to San Pablo and Suisun bays, through the maze of sloughs and islands above Antioch, Rio Vista, and the port of Stockton. For him a boat was a home away from home, and if the striped bass were running, it was all the excuse he needed to hail a friend, set the Roamer to sail, and head out where the action was. Here was a man who considered even the mishaps of piloting a small boat "to be punctuations of joy."

Jack and Charmian London with Laurie Godfrey-Smith on the *Roamer*.

SMALL-BOAT SAILING

A SAILOR IS BORN, NOT MADE. AND BY "SAILOR" IS MEANT, not the average efficient and hopeless creature who is found to-day in the forecastle of deepwater ships, but the man who will take a fabric compounded of wood and iron and rope and canvas and compel it to obey his will on the surface of the sea. Barring captains and mates of big ships, the small-boat sailor is the real sailor. He knows—he must know—how to make the wind carry his craft from one given point to another given point. He must know about tides and rips and eddies, bar and channel markings, and day and night signals; he must be wise in weather-lore; and he must be sympathetically familiar with the peculiar qualities of his boat which differentiate it from every other boat that was ever built and rigged. He must know how to gentle her about, as one instance of a myriad, and to fill her on the other tack without deadening her way or allowing her to fall off too far.

The deepwater sailor of to-day needs know none of these things. And he doesn't. He pulls and hauls as he is ordered, swabs decks, washes paint, and chips iron-rust. He knows nothing, and cares less. Put him in a small boat and he is helpless. He will cut an even better figure on the hurricane deck of a horse.

I shall never forget my child-astonishment when I first encountered one of these strange beings. He was a runaway English sailor. I was a lad of twelve, with a decked-over, fourteen-foot, centre-board skiff which I had taught myself to sail. I sat at his feet as at the feet of a god, while he discoursed of strange lands and peoples, deeds of violence, and hair-raising gales at sea. Then, one day, I took him for a sail. With all the trepidation of the veriest little amateur, I hoisted sail and got under way. Here was a man, looking on critically, I was sure, who knew more in one second about boats and the water than I could ever know. After an interval, in which I exceeded myself, he took the tiller and the sheet. I sat on the little thwart amidships, open-mouthed, prepared to learn what real sailing was. My mouth remained open, for I learned what a real sailor was in a small boat. He couldn't trim the sheet to save himself, he nearly capsized several times in squalls, and, once again, by blunderingly jibing over; he didn't know what a centre-board was for, nor did he know that in running a boat before the wind one must sit in the middle instead of on the side; and finally, when we came back to the wharf, he ran the skiff in full tilt, shattering her nose and carrying away the mast-step. And yet he was a really truly sailor fresh from the vasty deep.

Which points my moral. A man can sail in the forecastles of big ships all his life and never know what real sailing is. From the time I was twelve, I listened to the lure of the sea. When I was fifteen I was captain and owner of an oyster-pirate sloop. By the time I was sixteen I was sailing in scow-schooners, fishing salmon with the Greeks up the Sacramento River, and serving as sailor on the fish patrol. And I was a good sailor, too, though all my cruising had been on San Francisco Bay and the rivers tributary to it. I had never been on the ocean in my life.

Then, the month I was seventeen, I signed before the mast as an able seaman on a three-top-mast schooner bound on a seven-months' cruise across the Pacific and back again. As my shipmates promptly informed me, I had had my nerve with me to sign on as able seaman. Yet behold, I *was* an able seaman. I had graduated from the right school. It took no more than minutes to learn the names and uses of the few new ropes. It was simple. I did not do things blindly. As a small-boat sailor I had learned to reason out and know the *why* of everything. It is true, I had to learn how to steer by compass, which took maybe half a minute; but when it came to steering "full-and-by" and "close-and-by," I could beat the average of my shipmates, because that was the very way I had always sailed. Inside fifteen minutes I could box the compass around and back again. And there was little else to learn during that seven-months' cruise, except fancy rope-sailorising, such as the more complicated lanyard knots and the making of various kinds of sennit and rope-mats. The point of all of which is that it is by means of small-boat sailing that the real sailor is best schooled.

And if a man is a born sailor, and has gone to the school of the sea, never in all his life can he get away from the sea again. The salt of it is in his bones as well as his nostrils, and the sea will call to him until he dies. Of late years, I have found easier ways of earning a living. I have quit the forecastle for keeps, but always I come back to the sea. In my case it is usually San Francisco Bay, than which no lustier, tougher, sheet of water can be found for small-boat sailing.

It really blows on San Francisco Bay. During the winter, which is the best cruising season, we have southeasters, southwesters, and occasional howling northers. Throughout the summer we have what we call the "sea-breeze," an unfailing wind off the Pacific that on most afternoons in the week blows what the Atlantic Coast yachtsmen would name a gale. They are always surprised by the small spread of canvas our yachts carry. Some of them, with schooners they have sailed around the Horn, have looked proudly at their own lofty sticks and huge spreads, then patronisingly and even pityingly at ours. Then, perchance, they have joined a club cruise from San Francisco to Mare Island. They found the morning run up the Bay delightful. In the afternoon, when the brave west wind ramped across San Pablo Bay and they faced it on the long beat home, things were somewhat different. One by one, like a flight of swallows, our more meagrely sparred and canvassed yachts went by, leaving them wallowing and dead and shortening down in what they called a gale but which we called a dandy sailing breeze. The next time they came out, we would notice their sticks cut down, their booms shortened, and their after leeches nearer the luffs by whole cloths.

As for excitement, there is all the difference in the world between a ship in trouble at sea, and a small boat in trouble on land-locked water. Yet for genuine excitement and thrill, give me the small boat. Things happen so quickly, and there are always so few to do the work—and hard work, too, as the small-boat sailor knows. I have toiled all night, both watches on deck, in a typhoon off the coast of Japan, and been less exhausted than by two hours' work at reefing down a thirty-foot sloop and heaving up two anchors on a lee shore in a screaming southeaster.

Hard work and excitement? Let the wind baffle and drop in a heavy tide-way just as you are sailing your little sloop through a narrow drawbridge. Behold your sails, upon which you are depending, flap with sudden emptiness, and then see the impish wind, with a haul of eight points, fill your jib aback with a gusty puff. Around she goes, and sweeps, not through the open draw, but broadside on against the solid piles. Hear the roar of the tide, sucking through the trestle. And hear and see your pretty, fresh-painted boat crash against the piles. Feel her stout little hull give to the impact. See the rail actually pinch in. Hear your canvas tearing, and see the black, square-ended timbers thrusting holes through it. Smash! There goes your topmast stay, and the topmast reels over drunkenly above you. There is a ripping and crunching. If it continues, your starboard shrouds will be torn out. Grab a rope—any rope—and take a turn around a pile. But the free end of the rope is too short. You can't make it fast, and you hold on and wildly yell for your one companion to get a turn with another and longer rope. Hold on! You hold on till you

are purple in the face, till it seems your arms are dragging out of
their sockets, till the blood bursts from the ends of your fingers. But
you hold, and your partner gets the longer rope and makes it fast.
You straighten up and look at your hands. They are ruined. You
can scarcely relax the crooks of the fingers. The pain is sickening.
But there is no time. The skiff, which is always perverse, is pounding against the barnacles on the piles which threaten to scrape its
gunwale off. It's drop the peak! Down jib! Then you run lines, and
pull and haul and heave, and exchange unpleasant remarks with the
bridge-tender who is always willing to meet you more than half way
in such repartee. And finally, at the end of an hour, with aching
back, sweat-soaked shirt, and slaughtered hands, you are through
and swinging along on the placid, beneficent tide between narrow
banks where the cattle stand knee-deep and gaze wonderingly at you.
Excitement! Work! Can you beat it in a calm day on the deep sea?

I've tried it both ways. I remember labouring in a fourteen-days'
gale off the coast of New Zealand. We were a tramp collier, rusty
and battered, with six thousand tons of coal in our hold. Life lines
were stretched fore and aft; and on our weather side, attached to
smokestack guys and rigging, were huge rope-nettings, hung there
for the purpose of breaking the force of the seas and so saving our
mess-room doors. But the doors were smashed and the mess-rooms
washed out just the same. And yet, out of it all, arose but the one
feeling, namely, of monotony.

In contrast with the foregoing, about the liveliest eight days of my
life were spent in a small boat on the west coast of Korea. Never
mind why I was thus voyaging up the Yellow Sea during the month
of February in below-zero weather. The point is that I was in an
open boat, a *sampan*, on a rocky coast where there were no light-
houses and where the tides ran from thirty to sixty feet. My crew
was Japanese fishermen. We did not speak each other's language.
Yet there was nothing monotonous about that trip. Never shall I forget one particular cold bitter dawn, when, in the thick of driving
snow, we took in sail and dropped our small anchor. The wind was
howling out of the northwest, and we were on a lee shore. Ahead
and astern, all escape was cut off by rocky headlands, against whose
bases burst the unbroken seas. To windward a short distance, seen
only between the snow-squalls, was a low rocky reef. It was this
that inadequately protected us from the whole Yellow Sea that
thundered in upon us.

The Japanese crawled under a communal rice mat and went to
sleep. I joined them, and for several hours we dozed fitfully. Then
a sea deluged us out with icy water, and we found several inches

of snow on top the mat. The reef to windward was disappearing under the rising tide, and moment by moment the seas broke more strongly over the rocks. The fishermen studied the shore anxiously. So did I, and with a sailor's eye, though I could see little chance for a swimmer to gain that surf-hammered line of rocks. I made signs toward the headlands on either flank. The Japanese shook their heads. I indicated that dreadful lee shore. Still they shook their heads and did nothing. My conclusion was that they were paralysed by the hopelessness of the situation. Yet our extremity increased with every minute, for the rising tide was robbing us of the reef that served as buffer. It soon became a case of swamping at our anchor. Seas were splashing on board in growing volume, and we baled constantly. And still my fishermen crew eyed the surf-battered shore and did nothing.

At last, after many narrow escapes from complete swamping, the fishermen got into action. All hands tailed on to the anchor and hove it up. For'ard, as the boat's head paid off, we set a patch of sail about the size of a flour-sack. And we headed straight for shore. I unlaced my shoes, unbuttoned my great-coat and coat, and was ready to make a quick partial strip a minute or so before we struck. But we didn't strike, and, as we rushed in, I saw the beauty of the situation. Before us opened a narrow channel, frilled at its mouth with breaking seas. Yet, long before, when I had scanned the shore closely, there had been no such channel. *I had forgotten the thirty-foot tide.* And it was for this tide that the Japanese had so precariously waited. We ran the frill of breakers, curved into a tiny sheltered bay where the water was scarcely flawed by the gale, and landed on a beach where the salt sea of the last tide lay frozen in long curving lines. And this was one gale of three in the course of those eight days in the *sampan.* Would it have been beaten on a ship? I fear me the ship would have gone aground on the outlying reef and that its people would have been incontinently and monotonously drowned.

There are enough surprises and mishaps in a three-days' cruise in a small boat to supply a great ship on the ocean for a full year. I remember, once, taking out on her trial trip a little thirty-footer I had just bought. In six days we had two stiff blows, and, in addition, one proper southwester and one ripsnorting southeaster. The slight intervals between these blows were dead calms. Also, in the six days, we were aground three times. Then, too, we tied up to the bank in the Sacramento River, and, grounding by an accident on the steep slope on a falling tide, nearly turned a side somersault down the bank. In a stark calm and a heavy tide in the Carquinez Straits, where anchors skate on the channel-scoured bottom, we were sucked against a big dock and smashed and bumped down a quarter of a mile of its length before we could get clear. Two hours afterward, on San Pablo Bay, the wind was piping up and we were reefing down. It is no fun to pick up a skiff adrift in a heavy sea and gale. That was our next task, for our skiff, swamping, parted both towing painters we had bent on. Before we recovered it we had nearly killed ourselves with exhaustion, and we certainly had strained the sloop in every part from keelson to truck. And to cap it all, coming into our home port, beating up the narrowest part of the San Antonio Estuary, we had a shave of inches from collision with a big ship in tow of a tug. I have sailed the ocean in far larger craft a year at a time, in which period occurred no such chapter of moving incident.

After all, the mishaps are almost the best part of small-boat sailing. Looking back, they prove to be punctuations of joy. At the time they try your mettle and your vocabulary, and may make you so pessimistic as to believe that God has a grudge against you—but afterward, ah, afterward, with what pleasure you remember them and with what gusto do you relate them to your brother skippers in the fellowhood of small-boat sailing.

A narrow, winding slough; a half tide, exposing mud surfaced with gangrenous slime; the water itself filthy and discoloured by the waste from the vats of a near-by tannery; the marsh grass on either side molted with all the shades of a decaying orchid; a crazy, ramshackled, ancient wharf; and at the end of the wharf a small, white-painted sloop. Nothing romantic about it. No hint of adventure. A splendid pictorial argument against the alleged joys of small-boat sailing. Possibly that is what Cloudesley and I thought, that sombre, leaden morning as we turned out to cook breakfast and wash decks. The latter was my stunt, but one look at the dirty water overside, and another at my fresh-painted deck, deterred me. After breakfast, we started a game of chess. The tide continued to fall, and we felt the sloop begin to list. We played on until the chess men began to fall over. The list increased, and we went on deck. Bow-line and stern-line were drawn taut. As we looked the boat listed still farther with an abrupt jerk. The lines were now very taut.

"As soon as her belly touches the bottom she will stop," I said.

Cloudesley sounded with a boat hook along the outside.

"Seven feet of water," he announced. "The bank is almost up and down. The first thing that touches will be her mast when she turns bottom up."

An ominous, minute snapping noise came from the stern-line. Even as we looked, we saw a strand fray and part. Then we jumped.

Scarcely had we bent another line between the stern and the wharf, when the original line parted. As we bent another line for'ard, the original one there crackled and parted. After that, it was an inferno of work and excitement. We ran more and more lines, and more and more lines continued to part, and more and more the pretty boat went over on her side. We bent all our spare lines; we unrove sheets and halyards; we used our two-inch hawser; we fastened lines part way up the mast, half way up, and everywhere else. We toiled and sweated and enounced our mutual and sincere conviction that God's grudge still held against us. Country yokels came down on the wharf and sniggered at us. When Cloudesley let a coil of rope slip down the inclined deck into the vile slime and fished it out with seasick countenance, the yokels sniggered louder and it was all I could do to prevent him from climbing up on the wharf and committing murder.

By the time the sloop's deck was perpendicular, we had unbent the boom-lift from below, made it fast to the wharf, and, with the other end fast nearly to the mast-head, heaved it taut with block and tackle. The lift was of steel wire. We were confident that it could stand the strain, but we doubted the holding-power of the stays that held the mast.

The tide had two more hours to ebb (and it was the big run-out), which meant that five hours must elapse ere the returning tide would give us a chance to learn whether or not the sloop would rise to it and right herself. The bank was almost up and down, and at the bottom, directly beneath us, the fast-ebbing tide left a pit of the vilest, illest-smelling, illest-appearing muck to be seen in many a day's ride. Said Cloudesley to me gazing down into it:

"I love you as a brother. I'd fight for you. I'd face roaring lions, and sudden death by field and flood. But just the same, don't you fall into that." He shuddered nauseously. "For if you do, I haven't the grit to pull you out. I simply couldn't. You'd be awful. The best I could do would be to take a boat-hook and shove you down out of sight."

We sat on the upper side-wall of the cabin, dangled our legs down the top of the cabin, leaned our backs against the deck, and played chess until the rising tide and the block and tackle on the boom-lift enabled us to get her on a respectable keel again. Years afterward, down in the South Seas, on the island of Ysabel, I was caught in a similar predicament. In order to clean her copper, I had careened the *Snark* broadside on to the beach and outward. When the tide rose, she refused to rise. The water crept in through the scuppers, mounted over the rail, and the level of the ocean slowly crawled up the slant of the deck. We battened down the engine room hatch, and the sea rose to it and over it and climbed perilously near to the cabin companionway and skylight. We were all sick with fever, but we turned out in the blazing tropic sun and toiled madly for several hours. We carried our heaviest lines ashore from our mast-heads and heaved with our heaviest purchase until everything crackled including ourselves. We would spell off and lie down like dead men, then get up and heave and crackle again. And in the end, our lower rail five feet under water and the wavelets lapping the companionway combing, the sturdy little craft shivered and shook herself and pointed her masts once more to the zenith.

There is never lack of exercise in small-boat sailing, and the hard work is not only part of the fun of it, but it beats the doctors. San Francisco Bay is no mill pond. It is a large and draughty and variegated piece of water. I remember, one winter evening, trying to enter the mouth of the Sacramento. There was a freshet on the river, the flood tide from the bay had been beaten back into a strong ebb, and the lusty west wind died down with the sun. It was just sunset, and with a fair to middling breeze, dead aft, we stood still in the rapid current. We were squarely in the mouth of the river; but there was no anchorage and we drifted backward, faster and faster, and dropped anchor outside as the last breath of wind left us. The night came on, beautiful and warm and starry. My one companion cooked supper, while on deck I put everything in shape Bristol fashion. When we turned in at nine o'clock the weather-promise was excellent. (If I had carried a barometer I'd have known better.) By two in the morning our shrouds were thumming in a piping breeze, and I got up and gave her more scope on her hawser. Inside another hour there was no doubt that we were in for a southeaster.

It is not nice to leave a warm bed and get out of a bad anchorage in a black blowy night, but we arose to the occasion, put in two reefs, and started to heave up. The winch was old, and the strain of the jumping head sea was too much for it. With the winch out of commission, it was impossible to heave up by hand. We knew, because we tried it and slaughtered our hands. Now a sailor hates to lose an anchor. It is a matter of pride. Of course, we could have buoyed ours and slipped it. Instead, however, I gave her still more hawser, veered her, and dropped the second anchor.

There was little sleep after that, for first one and then the other of us would be rolled out of our bunks. The increasing size of the seas told us we were dragging, and when we struck the scoured channel we could tell by the feel of it that our two anchors were fairly skating across. It was a deep channel, the farther edge of it rising steeply like the wall of a canyon, and when our anchors started up that wall they hit in and held. Yet, when we fetched up, through the darkness we could hear the seas breaking on the solid shore astern, and so near was it that we shortened the skiff's painter.

Daylight showed us that between the stern of the skiff and destruction was no more than a score of feet. And how it did blow! There were times, in the gusts, when the wind must have approached a velocity of seventy or eighty miles an hour. But the anchors held, and so nobly that our final anxiety was that the for'ard bitts would be jerked clean out of the boat. All day the sloop alternately ducked her nose under and sat down on her stern; and it was not till late afternoon that the storm broke in one last and worst mad gust. For a full five minutes an absolute dead calm prevailed, and then, with the suddenness of a thunderclap, the wind snorted out of the southwest—a shift of eight points and a boisterous gale. Another night of it was too much for us, and we hove up by hand in a cross head-sea. It was not stiff work. It was heartbreaking. And I know we were both near to crying from the hurt and the exhaustion. And when we did get the first anchor up-and-down we couldn't break it out. Between seas we snubbed her nose down to it, took plenty of turns, and stood clear as she jumped. Almost everything smashed and parted except the anchor-hold. The chocks were jerked out, the rail torn off, and the very covering-board splintered, and still the anchor held. At last, hoisting the reefed mainsail and slacking off a few of the hard-won feet of the chain, we sailed the anchor out. It was nip and tuck, though, and there were times when the boat was knocked down flat. We repeated the maneuver with the remaining anchor, and in the gathering darkness fled into the shelter of the river's mouth.

I was born so long ago that I grew up before the era of gasoline. As a result, I am old-fashioned. I prefer a sail-boat to a motor-boat, and it is my belief that boat-sailing is a finer, more difficult, and sturdier art than running a motor. Gasoline engines are becoming fool proof, and while it is unfair to say that any fool can run an engine, it is fair to say that almost any one can. Not so, when it comes to sailing a boat. More skill, more intelligence, and a vast deal more training are necessary. It is the finest training in the world for boy and youth and man. If the boy is very small, equip him with a small, comfortable skiff. He will do the rest. He won't need to be taught. Shortly he will be setting a tiny leg-of-mutton and steering with an oar. Then he will begin to talk keels and centre-boards and want to take his blankets out and stop aboard all night.

But don't be afraid for him. He is bound to run risks and encoun-

123

ter accidents. Remember, there are accidents in the nursery as well as out on the water. More boys have died from hot-house culture than have died on boats large and small; and more boys have been made into strong and reliant men by boat-sailing than by lawn-cro-quet and dancing school.

And once a sailor, always a sailor. The savour of the salt never stales. The sailor never grows so old that he does not care to go back for one more wrestling bout with wind and wave. I know it of my-self. I have turned rancher, and live beyond sight of the sea. Yet I can stay away from it only so long. After several months have passed, I begin to grow restless. I find myself day-dreaming over incidents of the last cruise, or wondering if the striped bass are running on Wingo Slough, or eagerly reading the newspapers for reports of the first northern flights of ducks. And then, suddenly, there is a hur-ried packing of suit-cases and overhauling of gear, and we are off for Vallejo where the little *Roamer* lies, waiting, always waiting, for the skiff to come alongside, for the lighting of the fire in the galley-stove, for the pulling off of gaskets, the swinging up of the mainsail, and the rat-tat-tat of the reef-points, for the heaving short and the breaking out, and for the twirling of the wheel as she fills away and heads up Bay or down.

JACK LONDON

On Board *Roamer*,
   Sonoma Creek,
      April 15, 1911

9.

Navigating Four Horses North of the Bay

Prior to the Londons' departure for northwestern California on a 1,500-mile, four-horse trip in 1911, London wrote to an editor, "I am starting tomorrow morning with my wife on a three-months' driving trip. We have broken four saddle-horses, and are carrying our saddles with us as well. I dearly love California, so much so that you never see me East, and I shall gather up in these three months all sorts of data and atmosphere. . . ."

The "data and atmosphere" London referred to was background information he planned to use in the travel portions of The Valley of the Moon. But he went beyond gathering "local color" wherever he went. London was a disciplined professional, and he never left his work behind; he wrote even while away from home.

This trip was no exception, yet it provided the Londons with a much needed vacation (they were still recovering from the loss of their infant daughter, who had died shortly after birth nearly a year earlier) as well as an opportunity to explore a part of California neither had seen before. Aside from handling his four-horse team, fishing in the streams and the coastal waters, sailing, and cultivating new friendships along the way, London made time to write some stories, as well as this account of their trip, which was mailed to the editor of Sunset magazine when they reached Eureka.

In the heart of California's magnificent redwood empire.

NAVIGATING FOUR HORSES NORTH OF THE BAY

"HUH! DRIVE FOUR HORSES! I WOULDN'T SIT BEHIND YOU—not for a thousand dollars—over them mountain roads."

So said Henry, and he ought to have known, for he drives four horses himself.

Said another Glen Ellen friend: "What? London? He drive four horses? Can't drive one!"

And the best of it is that he was right. Even after managing to get a few hundred miles with my four horses, I don't know how to drive one. Just the other day, swinging down a steep mountain road and rounding an abrupt turn, I came full tilt on a horse and buggy being driven by a woman up the hill. We could not pass on the narrow road, where was only a foot to spare, and my horses did not know how to back, especially uphill. About two hundred yards down the hill was a spot where we could pass. The driver of the buggy said she didn't dare back down because she was not sure of the brake. And as I didn't know how to tackle one horse, I didn't try it. So we unhitched her horse and backed down by hand. Which was very well, till it came to hitching the horse to the buggy again. She didn't know how. I didn't either, and I had depended on her knowledge. It took us about half an hour, with frequent debates and consultations, though it is an absolute certainty that never in its life was that horse hitched in that particular way.

No; I can't harness up one horse. But I can four, which compels me to back up again to get to my beginning. Having selected Sonoma Valley for our abiding place, Charmian and I decided it was about time we knew what we had in our own country and the neighboring ones. How to do it, was the first question. Among our many weaknesses is the one of being old-fashioned. We don't mix with gasoline very well. And, as true sailors should, we naturally gravitate toward horses. Being one of those lucky individuals who carries his office under his hat, I should have to take a typewriter and a load of books along. This put saddle-horses out of the running. Charmian suggested driving a span. She had faith in me; besides, she could drive a span herself. But when I thought of the many mountains to cross, and of crossing them for three months with a poor tired span, I vetoed the proposition and said we'd have to come back to gasoline after all. This she vetoed just as emphatically, and a deadlock obtained until I received inspiration.

"Why not drive four horses?" I said.

"But you don't know how to drive four horses" was her objection.

I threw my chest out and my shoulders back. "What man has done, I can do," I proclaimed grandly. "And please don't forget that when we sailed on the Snark I knew nothing of navigation, and that I taught myself as I sailed."

"Very well," she said. (And there's faith for you!) "They shall be four saddle-horses, and we'll strap our saddles on behind the rig."

It was my turn to object. "Our saddle-horses are not broken to harness."

"Then break them."

And what I knew about horses, much less about breaking them, was just about as much as any sailor knows. Having been kicked, bucked off, fallen over backward upon, and thrown out and run over, on very numerous occasions, I had a mighty vigorous respect for horses; but a wife's faith must be lived up to, and I went at it.

King was a polo pony from St. Louis, and Prince a many-gaited love-horse from Pasadena. The hardest thing was to get them to dig in and pull. They frollicked along on the levels and galloped down the hills, but when they struck an up-grade and felt the weight of the breaking-cart, they stopped and turned around and looked at me. But I passed them, and my troubles began. Milda was fourteen years old, an unadulterated bronco, and in temperament was a combination of mule and jack-rabbit blended equally. If you pressed your hand on her flank and told her to get over, she lay down on you. If you got her by the head and told her to back, she walked forward over you. And if you got behind her and shoved and told her to "Giddap!" she sat down on you. Also, she wouldn't walk. For endless weary miles I strove with her, but never could I get her to walk a step. Finally, she was a manger-glutton. No matter how near or far from the stable, when six o'clock came around she bolted for home and never missed the directest cross-road. Many times I rejected her.

The fourth and most rejected horse of all was the Outlaw. From the age of three to seven she had defied all horse-breakers and broken a number of them. Then a long lanky cowboy, with a fifty-pound saddle and a Mexican bit, had got her proud goat. I was the next owner. She was my favorite riding-horse. Charmian said I'd have to put her in as a wheeler where I would have more control over her. Now Charmian had a favorite riding mare called Maid. I suggested Maid as a substitute. Charmian pointed out that my mare was a branded range horse, while hers was a thoroughbred, and that the legs of her mare would be ruined forever if she were driven for three months. I acknowledged her mare's thoroughbredness, and at the same time defied her to find any thoroughbred with as small and delicately-viciously pointed ears as my Outlaw. She indicated Maid's exquisitely thin shin-bone. I measured the Outlaw's. It was equally thin, although, I insinuated, possibly more durable. This stabbed Charmian's pride. Of course her thoroughbred Maid, carrying the blood of "Old Lexington, Morella, and a streak of the super-enduring Morgan," could run, walk, and work my unregistered Outlaw into the ground; and that was the very precise reason why such a paragon of a saddle animal should not be degraded by harness.

So it was that Charmian remained obdurate, until, one day, I got her behind the Outlaw for a forty-mile drive. For every inch of those forty miles the Outlaw kicked and jumped, in between the kicks and jumps finding time and space in which to seize its team-mate by the back of the neck and attempt to drag it to the ground. Another trick the Outlaw developed during that drive was suddenly to turn at right angles in the traces and endeavor to butt its team-mate over the grade. Reluctantly and nobly did Charmian give in and consent to the use of Maid. The Outlaw's shoes were pulled off, and she was turned out on the range.

Finally, the four horses were hooked to the rig—a light Studebaker trap. With two hours and a half of practice, in which the excitement was not abated by several jack-poles and numerous kicking matches, I announced myself as ready for the start. Came the morning, and Prince, who was to have been a wheeler with Maid, showed up with a badly kicked shoulder. He did not exactly show up; we had to find him, for he was unable to walk. His leg swelled and continually swelled during the several days we waited for him. Remained only the Outlaw. In from pasture she came, shoes were nailed on, and she was harnessed into the wheel. Friends and relatives strove to press accident policies on me, but Charmian climbed up alongside, and Nakata got into the rear seat with the typewriter—Nakata, who sailed cabin-boy on the Snark for two years and who has shown himself afraid of nothing, not even of me and my amateur jamborees in experimenting with new modes of locomo-

129

tion. And we did very nicely, thank you, especially after the first hour or so, during which time the Outlaw had kicked about fifty various times, chiefly to the damage of her own legs and the paint-work, and after she had bitten a couple of hundred times, to the damage of Maid's neck and Charmian's temper. It was hard enough to have her favorite mare in the harness without also enduring the spectacle of its being eaten alive.

Our leaders were joys. King being a polo pony and Milda a rabbit, they rounded curves beautifully and darted ahead like coyotes out of the way of the wheelers. Milda's besetting weakness was a fran-tic desire not to have the lead-bar strike her hocks. When this hap-pened, one of three things occurred: either she sat down on the lead-bar, kicked it up in the air until she got her back under it, or ex-ploded in a straight-ahead, harness-disrupting jump. Not until she carried the lead-bar clean away and danced a breakdown on it and the traces, did she behave decently. Nakata and I made the repairs with good old-fashioned bale-rope, which is stronger than wrought-iron any time, and we went on our way.

In the meantime I was learning—I shall not say to tool a four-in-hand—but just simply to drive four horses. Now it is all right enough to begin with four work-horses pulling a load of several tons. But to begin with four light horses, all running, and a light rig that seems to outrun them—well, when things happen they happen quickly. My weakness was total ignorance. In particular, my fingers lacked training, and I made the mistake of depending on my eyes to han-dle the reins. This brought me up against a disastrous optical illu-sion. The bight of the off lead-line, being longer and heavier than that of the off wheel-line, hung lower. In a moment requiring quick action, I invariably mistook the two lines. Pulling on what I thought was the wheel-line, in order to straighten the team, I would see the leaders swing abruptly around into a jack-pole. Now for sensations of sheer impotence, nothing can compare with a jack-pole, when the horrified driver beholds his leaders prancing gaily up the road and his wheelers jogging steadily down the road, all at the same time and all harnessed together and to the same rig.

I no longer jack-pole, and I don't mind admitting how I got out of the habit. It was my eyes that enslaved my fingers into ill-practices. So I shut my eyes and let the fingers go it alone. Today my fingers are independent of my eyes and work automatically. I do not see what my fingers do. They just do it. All I see is the satisfactory re-sult.

Still we managed to get over the ground that first day—down sunny Sonoma Valley to the old town to Sonoma, founded by General Vallejo as the remotest outpost on the northern frontier for the purpose of holding back the Gentiles, as the wild Indians of those days were called. Here history was made. Here the last Spanish mission was reared; here the Bear flag was raised; and here Kit Carson, and Frémont, and all our early adventurers, came and rested in the days before the days of gold.

We swung on over the low rolling hills, through miles of dairy farms and chicken ranches where every blessed hen is white, and down the slopes to Petaluma Valley. Here, in 1776, Captain Quiros came up Petaluma Creek from San Pablo Bay in quest of an outlet to Bodega Bay on the coast. And here, later, the Russians, with Alaskan hunters, carried skin boats across from Fort Ross to poach for sea-otters on the Spanish preserve of San Francisco Bay. Here, too, still later, General Vallejo built a fort, which still stands—one of the finest examples of Spanish adobe that remain to us. And here, at the old fort, to bring the chronicle up to date, our horses proceeded to make peculiarly personal history with astonishing success and dispatch. King, our peerless polo-pony leader, went lame. So hopelessly lame did he go that no expert, then and afterward, could determine whether the lameness was in his frogs, hoofs, legs, shoulders, or head. Maid picked up a nail and began to limp. Milda, figuring the day already sufficiently spent and maniacal with manger gluttony, began to rabbit-jump. All that held her was the bale-rope. And the Outlaw, game to the last, exceeded all previous exhibitions of skin-removing, paint-marring, and horse-eating.

At Petaluma we rested over while King was returned to the ranch and Prince sent to us. Now Prince had proved himself an excellent wheeler, yet he had to go into the lead and let the Outlaw retain his old place. There is an axiom that a good wheeler is a poor leader. I object to the last adjective. A good wheeler makes an infinitely worse kind of a leader than that. I know . . . now. I ought to know. Since that day I have driven Prince a few hundred miles in the lead. He is neither any better nor any worse than the first mile he ran in the lead; and his worst is even extremely worse than what you are thinking. Not that he is vicious. He is merely a good-natured rogue who shakes hands for sugar, steps on your toes out of sheer excessive friendliness, and just goes on loving you in your harshest moments.

But he won't get out of the way. Also, whenever he is reproved for being in the wrong, he accuses Milda of it and bites the back of her neck. So bad has this become that whenever I yell "Prince!" in a loud voice, Milda immediately rabbit-jumps to the side, straight ahead, or sits down on the lead-bar. All of which is quite disconcerting. Picture it yourself. You are swinging a sharp, down-grade, mountain curve, at a fast trot. The rock wall is the outside of the curve. The inside of the curve is a precipice. The continuance of the curve is a narrow unrailed bridge. You hit the curve, throwing the leaders in against the wall and making the pole-horse do the work. All is lovely. The leaders are hugging the wall like nestling doves. But the moment comes in the evolution when the leaders must shoot out ahead. They really must shoot, or else they'll hit the wall and miss the bridge. Also, behind them are the wheelers, and the rig, and you have just eased the brake in order to put sufficient snap into the maneuver. If ever team-work is required, now is the time. Milda tries to shoot. She does her best, but Prince, bubbling over with roguishness, lags behind. He knows the trick. Milda is half a length ahead of him. He times it to the fraction of a second. Maid, in the wheel, over-running him, naturally bites him. This disturbs the Outlaw, who has been behaving beautifully, and she immediately reaches across for Maid. Simultaneously, with a fine display of firm conviction that it's all Milda's fault, Prince sinks his teeth into the back of Milda's defenseless neck. The whole thing has occurred in less than a second. Under the surprise and pain of the bite, Milda either jumps ahead to the imminent peril of harness and lead-bar, or smashes into the wall, stops short with the lead-bar over her back, and emits a couple of hysterical kicks. The Outlaw invariably selects this moment to remove paint. And after things are untangled and you have had time to appreciate the close shave, you go up to Prince and reprove him with your choicest vocabulary. And Prince, gazelle-eyed and tender, offers to shake hands with you for sugar. I leave it to any one: a boat would never act that way.

We have some history north of the bay. Nearly three centuries and a half ago, that doughty pirate and explorer, Sir Francis Drake, combing the Pacific for Spanish galleons, anchored in the bight formed by Point Reyes, on which today is one of the richest dairy regions in the world. Here, less than two decades after Drake, Sebastien Carmenon piled up on the rocks with a silkladen galleon from the Philippines. And in this same bay of Drake, long afterward, the Russian fur-poachers rendezvoused their *bidarkas* and stole in through the Golden Gate to the forbidden waters of San Francisco Bay.

Farther up the coast, in Sonoma County, we pilgrimaged to the sites of the Russian settlements. At Bodega Bay, south of what today is called Russian River, was their anchorage, while north of the river they built their fort. And much of Fort Ross still stands. Log-bastions, church, and stables hold their own, and so well, with rusty hinges creaking, that we warmed ourselves at the hundred-years-old double fireplace and slept under the hand-hewn roof beams still held together by spikes of hand-wrought iron.

We went to see where history had been made, and we saw scenery as well. One of our stretches in a day's drive was from beautiful Inverness on Tomales Bay, down the Olema Valley to Bolinas Bay, along the eastern shore of that body of water to Willow Camp, and up over the sea-bluffs, around the bastions of Tamalpais, and down to Sausalito. From the head of Bolinas Bay to Willow Camp the drive on the edge of the beach, and actually, for half-mile stretches, in the waters of the bay itself, was a delightful experience. The wonderful part was to come. Very few San Franciscans, much less Californians, know of that drive from Willow Camp, to the south and east, along the poppy-blown cliffs, with the sea thundering in the sheer depths hundreds of feet below and the Golden Gate opening up ahead, disclosing smoky San Francisco on her many hills. Far off, blurred on the breast of the sea, can be seen the Farallones, which Sir Francis Drake passed on a southwest course in the thick of a fog that robbed him of the glory of discovering San Francisco Bay.

It was on this part of the drive that I decided at last I was learning real mountain-driving. To confess the truth, for delicious titillation of one's nerve, I have since driven over no mountain road that was worse, or better, rather, than that piece.

And then the contrast! From Sausalito, over excellent parklike boulevards, through the splendid redwoods and homes of Mill Valley, across the blossomed hills of Marin County, along the knoll-studded picturesque marshes, past San Rafael resting warmly among her hills, over the divide and up the Petaluma Valley, and on to the grassy feet of Sonoma Mountain and home. We covered fifty-five miles that day. Not so bad, eh, for Prince the Rogue, the paint-removing Outlaw, the thin-shanked thoroughbred, and the rabbit-jumper? And they came in cool and dry, ready for their mangers and the straw.

Oh, we didn't stop. We considered we were just starting, and that was many weeks ago. We have kept on, going over six counties which are comfortably large, even for California, and we are still going. We have twisted and doubled, crisscrossed our tracks, made fascinating and lengthy dives into the interior valleys in the hearts of Napa and Lake counties, traveled the coast for hundreds of miles on end, and are now in Eureka, on Humboldt Bay, which was discovered by accident by the gold-seekers, who were trying to find their way to and from the Trinity diggings. Even here, the white man's history preceded them, for dim tradition says that the Russians once anchored

133

here and hunted sea-otter before the first Yankee trader rounded the Horn, or the first Rocky Mountain trapper thirsted across the "Great American Desert" and trickled down the snowy Sierra to the sun-kissed land. No; we are not resting our horses here on Humboldt Bay. We are writing this, gorging on abalones and mussels, digging clams, and catching record-breaking sea-trout and rock-cod in the intervals in which we are not sailing, motor-boating, and swimming in the most temperately equable climate we have ever experienced.

These comfortably large counties! They are veritable empires. Take Humboldt, for instance. It is three times as large as Rhode Island, one and one half times as large as Delaware, almost as large as Connecticut, and half as large as Massachusetts. The pioneer has done his work in this north-of-the-bay region, the foundations are laid, and all is ready for the inevitable inrush of population and adequate development of resources which so far have been no more than skimmed, and casually and carelessly skimmed at that. This region of the six counties alone will some day support a population of millions. In the meanwhile, O you homeseekers, you wealth-seekers, and, above all, you climate-seekers, now is the time to get in on the ground floor.

Robert Ingersoll once said that the genial climate of California would in a fairly brief time evolve a race resembling the Mexicans, and that in two or three generations the Californians would be seen of a Sunday morning on their way to a cockfight with a rooster under each arm. Never was made a rasher generalization, based on so absolute an ignorance of facts. It is to laugh. Here is a climate that breeds vigor, with just sufficient geniality to prevent the expenditure of most of that vigor in fighting the elements. Here is a climate where a man can work three hundred and sixty-five days in the year without the slightest hint of enervation, and where for three hundred and sixty-five nights he must perforce sleep under blankets. What more can one say? I consider myself somewhat of a climate expert, having adventured among most of the climates of five out of the six zones. I have not yet been in the Antarctic, but whatever climate obtains there will not deter me from drawing the conclusion that nowhere is there a climate to compare with that of this region. Maybe I am as wrong as Ingersoll was. Nevertheless I take my medicine by continuing to live in this climate. Also, it is the only medicine I ever take.

But to return to the horses. There is some improvement. Milda has actually learned to walk. Maid has proved her thoroughbredness by never tiring on the longest days, and, while being the strongest and highest spirited of all, by never causing any trouble save for an occasional kick at the Outlaw. And the Outlaw rarely gallops, no longer butts, only periodically kicks, comes in to the pole and does her work without attempting to vivisect Maid's medulla oblongata, and—marvel of marvels—is really and truly getting lazy. But Prince remains the same incorrigible, loving and lovable rogue as always.

And the country we've been over! The drives through Napa and Lake counties! One, from Sonoma Valley, via Santa Rosa, we could not refrain from taking several ways, and on all the ways we found the roads excellent for machines as well as horses. One route, and a more delightful one for an automobile cannot be found, is out from Santa Rosa, past old Altruria and Mark West Springs, then to the right and across to Calistoga in Napa Valley. By keeping to the left, the drive holds on up the Russian River Valley, through the miles of the noted Asti vineyards to Cloverdale, and then by way of Pieta, Witter, and Highland Springs to Lakeport. Still another way we took was down Sonoma Valley, skirting San Pablo Bay, and up the lovely Napa Valley. From Napa were side excursions through Pope and Berryessa valleys, on to Aetna Springs, and into Lake County, crossing the famous Langtry Ranch.

More valley from Ukiah to Willits, and then we turned westward through the virgin Sherwood forest of magnificent redwood, stopping at Alpine for the night and continuing on through Mendocino County to Fort Bragg and "salt water." We also came to Fort Bragg up the coast from Fort Ross, keeping our coast journey intact from the Golden Gate. The coast weather was cool and delightful, the coast driving superb. Especially in the Fort Ross section did we find the roads thrilling, while all the way along we followed the sea. At every stream the road skirted dizzy cliff-edges, dived down into lush growths of forest and ferns, and climbed out along the cliff-edges again. The way was lined with flowers—wild lilac, wild roses, poppies, and lupins. Such lupins!—giant clumps of them of every lupin-shade and color. And it was along the Mendocino roads that Charmian caused many delays by insisting on getting out to pick the wild blackberries, strawberries, and thimbleberries which grew so profusely. And ever we caught peeps, far down, of steam schooners loading lumber in the rocky coves; ever we skirted the cliffs, day after day, crossing stretches of rolling farm lands and passing through thriving villages and saw-mill towns. Memorable was our launch-trip from Mendocino City up Big River, where the steering gears of the launches work the reverse of anywhere else in the world; where we saw a stream of logs, of six to twelve and fifteen feet in diameter, which filled the riverbed for miles to the obliteration of any sign of water; and where we were told of a white or albino redwood tree. We did not see this last, so cannot vouch for it.

All the streams were filled with trout, and more than once we saw side-hill salmon on the slopes. No, side-hill salmon is not a peripatetic fish; it is a deer out of season. But the trout! At Gualala Charmian caught her first one. Once before in my life I had caught two . . . on angleworms. On occasion I had tried fly and spinner and never got a strike, and I had come to believe that all this talk of fly-fishing was just so much nature-faking. But on the Gualala River I caught trout—a lot of them—on fly and spinner; and I was beginning to feel quite an expert, until Nakata, fishing on bottom with a pellet of bread for bait, caught the biggest trout of all. I now affirm there is nothing in science nor in art. Nevertheless, since that day poles and baskets have been added to our baggage, we tackle every stream we come to, and we no longer are able to remember the grand total of our catch.

At Usal, many hilly and picturesque miles north of Fort Bragg, we turned again into the interior of Mendocino, crossing the ranges and coming out in Humboldt County on the south fork of Eel River at Garberville. Throughout the trip, from Marin County north, we had been warned of "bad roads ahead." Yet we never found those bad roads. We seemed always to be just ahead of them or behind them. The farther we came the better the roads seemed, though this was probably due to the fact that we were learning more and more what four horses and a light rig could do on a road. And thus do I save my face with all the counties. I refuse to make invidious road comparisons. I can add that while, save in rare instances on steep pitches, I have trotted my horses down all the grades, I have never had one horse fall down nor have I had to send the rig to a blacksmith shop for repairs.

Also, I am learning to throw leather. If any tyro thinks it is easy to take a short-handled, long-lashed whip, and throw the end of that lash just where he wants it, let him put on automobile goggles and try it. On reconsideration, I would suggest the substitution of a wire fencing-mask for the goggles. For days I looked at that whip. It fascinated me, and the fascination was composed mostly of fear. At my first attempt, Charmian and Nakata became afflicted with the same fascination, and for a long time afterward, whenever they saw me reach for the whip, they closed their eyes and shielded their heads with their arms.

Here's the problem. Instead of pulling honestly, Prince is lagging back and maneuvering for a bite at Milda's neck. I have four reins in my hands. I must put these four reins into my left hand, properly gather the whip handle and the bight of the lash in my right hand, and throw that lash past Maid without striking her and into Prince. If the lash strikes Maid, her thoroughbredness will go up in the air and I'll have a case of horse hysteria on my hands for the next half hour. But follow. The whole problem is not yet stated. Suppose that I miss Maid and reach the intended target. The instant the lash cracks, the four horses jump, Prince most of all, and his jump, with spread wicked teeth, is for the back of Milda's neck. She jumps to escape— which is her second jump, for the first one came when the lash exploded. The Outlaw reaches for Maid's neck, and Maid, who has already jumped and tried to bolt, tries to bolt harder. And all this infinitesimal fraction of time I am trying to hold the four animals with my left hand, while my whip-lash, writhing through the air, is coming back to me. Three simultaneous things I must do: keep hold of the four lines with my left hand; slam on the brake with my foot; and on the rebound catch that flying lash in the hollow of my right arm and get the bight of it safely into my right hand. Then I must get two of the four lines back into my right hand and keep the horses from running away or going over the grade. Try it some time. You will find life anything but wearisome. Why, the first time I hit the mark and made the lash go off like a revolver shot, I was so astounded and delighted that I was paralyzed. I forgot to do any of the multitudinous other things, tangled the whip-lash in Maid's harness, and was forced to call upon Charmian for assistance. And now, confession. I carry a few pebbles handy. They're great for reaching Prince in a tight place. But just the same I'm learning that whip every day, and before I get home I hope to discard the pebbles. And as long as I rely on pebbles, I cannot truthfully speak of myself as "tooling a four-in-hand."

From Garberville, where we ate eel to repletion and got acquainted with the aborigines, we drove down the Eel River Valley for two days through the most unthinkably glorious body of redwood timber to be seen anywhere in California. From Dyerville on to Eureka we caught glimpses of railroad construction and of great concrete bridges in the course of building, which advertised that at last Humboldt County is to be linked to the rest of the world.

We still consider our trip is just begun. As soon as this is mailed from Eureka, it's heigh-ho! for the horses and pull on. We shall continue up the coast, turn in for the Hoopa Reservation and the gold mines, and shoot down the Trinity and Klamath rivers in Indian canoes to Requa. After that, we shall go on through Del Norte County and into Oregon. The trip so far has justified us in taking the attitude that we won't go home until the winter rains drive us in. And, finally, I am going to try the experiment of putting the Outlaw in the lead and relegating Prince to his old position in the near wheel. I won't need any pebbles then.

10.

"The Octopus"

A REVIEW OF FRANK NORRIS'S NOVEL

Jack London and Frank Norris were California contemporaries—
writers who at one time lived on opposite shores of San Francisco
Bay. Ironically, they never met. And judging from the lack of evidence, they never engaged in correspondence.

Though from vastly different social and economic back-
grounds—Norris came from a well-to-do, socially prominent family, while London was born and raised in a working-class environment—there were some striking parallels in their lives. They both
attended the University of California at Berkeley as special stu-
dents in the 1890s and each disliked their English classes; both were
influenced by the works of Rudyard Kipling; they were interested
in social reform; and they each used California as a backdrop for a
good portion of their fiction. Unfortunately, Norris's career was cut
short by his untimely death in 1902, when he was only thirty-two
years old.

While London was a relatively unknown writer when The Octopus was published in 1901, Norris, with the publication of his powerful novel about the clash between the California wheat growers
and the monopolistic railroad, was on the threshold of wide public
acclaim.

London had been monitoring his fellow writer's career; in 1899
he applauded Norris's Moran of the Lady Letty: A Story of Adventure Off the California Coast. In 1914 he sent an enthusiastic tele-
gram to Frank's brother, Charles, when the posthumous novel Vandover and the Brute appeared. In praise of Vandover, he wired: ". . .
it is all his ripe promise which he so splendidly fulfilled . . . all
lovers of Frank Norris will hail it with deepest satisfaction." And
he was no less generous in his acclaim for The Octopus in his exuberant review, which appeared in the June 1901 issue of Impressions.

Frank Norris, *ca.* 1902. London was a great admirer of his work. *Photograph courtesy of The Bancroft Library, University of California, Berkeley*

"THE OCTOPUS"

There it was, the Wheat, the Wheat! The little seed long planted, germinating in the deep, dark furrows of the soil, straining, swelling, suddenly in one night had burst upward to the light. The wheat had come up. It was before him, around him, everywhere, illimitable, immeasurable. The winter brownness of the ground was overlaid with a little shimmer of green. The promise of the sowing was being fulfilled. The earth, the loyal mother who never failed, who never disappointed, was keeping her faith again.

VERY LONG AGO, WE OF THE WEST HEARD IT RUMORED THAT Frank Norris had it in mind to write the *Epic of the Wheat*. Nor can it be denied that many of us doubted—not the ability of Frank Norris merely, but the ability of the human, of all humans. This great, incoherent, amorphous West! Who could grip the spirit and the essence of it, the luster and the wonder, and bind it all, definitely and sanely, within the covers of a printed book? Surely we of the West, who knew our West, may have been pardoned our lack of faith.

And now Frank Norris has done it; has, in a machine age, achieved what has been peculiarly the privilege of the man who lived in an heroic age; in short, has sung the *Epic of the Wheat*. "More power to his elbow," as Charles F. Lummis would say.

On first sight of the Valley of the San Joaquin, one can not help but call it the "new and naked land." There is apparently little to be seen. A few isolated ranches in the midst of the vastness, no timber, a sparse population—that is all. And the men of the ranches, sweating in bitter toil, they must likewise be new and naked. So it would seem; but Norris has given breadth to both, and depth. Not only has he gone down into the soil, into the womb of the passionate earth, yearning for motherhood, the sustenance of nations; but he has gone down into the heart of its people, simple, elemental, prone to the ruder amenities of existence, growling and snarling with brute anger under cruel wrong. One needs must feel a sympathy for these men, workers and fighters, and for all of their weakness, a respect. And, after all, as Norris has well shown, their weakness is

141

not inherent. It is the weakness of unorganization, the weakness of the force which they represent and of which they are a part, the agricultural force as opposed to the capitalistic force, the farmer against the financier, the tiller of the soil against the captain of industry.

No man, not large of heart, lacking in spontaneous sympathy, incapable of great enthusiasms, could have written The Octopus.[1] Presley, the poet, dreamer, and singer, is a composite fellow. So far as mere surface incident goes, he is audaciously Edwin Markham; but down in the heart of him he is Frank Norris. Presley, groping vaguely in the silence of the burning night for the sigh of the land; Presley, with his great Song of the West forever leaping up in his imagination and forever eluding him; Presley, wrestling passionately for the swing of his "thundering progression of hexameters"— who is this Presley but Norris, grappling in keen travail with his problem of The Octopus, and doubting often, as we of the West have doubted?

Men obtain knowledge in two ways: by generalizing from experience; by gathering to themselves the generalizations of others. As regards Frank Norris, one can avoid pausing for speculation. It is patent that in this, his last and greatest effort, he has laid down uncompromisingly the materialistic conception of history, or, more politely, the economic interpretation of history. Now the question arises: Did Frank Norris acquire the economic interpretation of history from the printed records of the thoughts of other men, and thus equipped, approach his problem of The Octopus? Or, rather, did he approach it, naïve and innocent? And from direct contact with the great social forces was he not forced to so generalize for himself? It is a pretty question. Will he some day tell us?

Did Norris undergo the same evolution he has so strongly depicted in Presley? Presley's ultimate sociological concept came somewhat in this fashion: Shelgrim, the president and owner of the Pacific and Southwestern, laid "a thick, powerful forefinger on the table to emphasize his words. 'Try to believe this—to begin with— that railroads build themselves. Where there is a demand, sooner or later there will be a supply. Mr. Derrick, does he grow his wheat? The wheat grows itself. What does he count for? Does he supply the force? What do I count for? Do I build the railroad? You are dealing with forces, young man, when you speak of wheat and the railroads, not with men. There is the wheat, the supply. It must be carried to feed the people. There is the demand. The wheat is one force, the railroad another, and there is the law that governs them—sup-

[1] The Octopus. By Frank Norris. New York, Doubleday, Page & Co., 1901.

ply and demand. Men have only little to do in the whole business. Complications may arise, conditions that bear hard on the individual—crush him, maybe—but the wheat will be carried to feed the people as inevitably as it will grow.' "

One feels disposed to quarrel with Norris for his inordinate realism. What does the world care whether Hooven's meat safe be square or oblong; whether it be lined with wire screen or mosquito netting; whether it be hung to the branches of the oak tree or to the ridgepole of the barn; whether, in fact, Hooven has a meat safe or not? "Feels disposed" is used advisedly. In truth, we can not quarrel with him. It is confession and capitulation. The facts are against us. He *has* produced results, Titanic results. Never mind the realism, the unimportant detail, minute description, Hooven's meat safe and the rest. Let it be stated flatly that by no other method could Frank Norris or anybody else have handled the vast Valley of the San Joaquin and the no less vast-tentacled *Octopus*. Results? It was the only way to get results, the only way to paint the broad canvas he has painted, with the sunflare in his brush.

But he gives us something more than realism. Listen to this:

Once more the pendulum of the seasons swung in its mighty arc.

Then, faint and prolonged, across the levels of the ranch, he heard the engine whistling for Bonneville. Again and again, at rapid intervals in its flying course, it whistled for road crossings, for sharp curves, for trestles; ominous notes, hoarse, bellowing, ringing with the accents of menace and defiance; and abruptly Presley saw again, in his imagination, the galloping monster, the terror of steel and steam, with its single eye, cyclopean, red, shooting from horizon to horizon; but saw it now as the symbol of a vast power, huge, terrible, flinging the echo of its thunder over all the reaches of the valley, leaving blood and destruction in its path; the leviathan, with tentacles of steel clutching into the soil, the soulless Force, the iron-hearted Power, the monster, the Colossus, the Octopus.

The direct brutality of ten thousand acres of wheat, nothing but wheat as far as the eye could see, stunned her a little. There was something vaguely indecent in the sight, this food of the people, this elemental force, this basic energy, weltering here under the sun in all the unconscious nakedness of a sprawling, primordial Titan.

Everywhere throughout the great San Joaquin, unseen and unheard, a thousand ploughs up-stirred the land, tens of thousands of shears clutched deep into the warm, moist soil. It was the long, stroking caress, vigorous, male, powerful, for which the Earth seemed panting. The heroic embrace of a multitude of iron hands, gripping down into the brown, warm flesh of the land that quivered responsive and passionate under this rude advance, so robust as to be almost an assault, so violent as to be veritably brutal. There, under the sun and under the speckless sheen of the sky, the wooing of the Titan began, the vast primal passion, the two world-forces, the elemental Male and Female, locked in a colossal embrace, at grapples in the throes of an infinite desire, at once terrible and divine, knowing no law, untamed, savage, natural, sublime.

Many men, and women, too, pass through the pages of *The Octopus*, but one, greatest of all, we can not forbear mentioning in passing—Annixter. Annixter, rough almost to insolence, direct in speech, intolerant in his opinions, relying upon absolutely no one but himself; crusty of temper, bullying of disposition, a ferocious worker, and as widely trusted as he was widely hated; obstinate and contrary, cantankerous, and deliciously afraid of "feemale women"—this is Annixter. He is worth knowing. In such cunning fashion has Norris blown the breath of life into him, that his death comes with a shock which is seldom produced by deaths in fiction. Osterman, laying his head on his arms like a tired man going to rest, and Delaney, crawling instinctively out of the blood-welter to die in the growing wheat; but it is Annixter, instantly killed, falling without movement, for whom we first weep. A living man there died.

Well, the promise of *Moran* and *McTeague* has been realized. Can we ask more? Yet we have only the first of the trilogy. *The Epic of the Wheat* is no little thing. Content with *The Octopus*, we may look forward to *The Pit* and *The Wolf*. We shall not doubt this time.

11.

The Story of an Eyewitness

A REPORT OF THE SAN FRANCISCO EARTHQUAKE OF APRIL 18, 1906

Shortly after five a.m. on April 18, Jack and Charmian London were shaken from sleep at Wake Robin Lodge in Glen Ellen by a temblor such as neither of the quake-conscious Californians had ever experienced. Half an hour later, they watched from a hillside on their ranch as columns of smoke rose from the smoldering ruins of San Francisco, forty miles away. Charmian remembered Jack exclaiming, "I shouldn't wonder if San Francisco had sunk. That was some earthquake. We don't know but the Atlantic may be washed up at the foot of the Rocky Mountains."

The Londons wasted little time and were soon in the midst of the rubble of San Francisco—talking to survivors and rescue workers, surveying the damage, and taking photographs of the devastated city. London's vivid report appeared in the May 5 issue of Collier's Weekly.

On June 2, 1906, it was reprinted in the Argonaut. The editors assigned it a lengthy and sensational descriptive title, characteristic of the times: "Jack London tells of the fire. San Francisco's burning. A lurid tower visible from afar. The deserted heart of San Francisco. The flight before the flames."

San Francisco after the devastating earthquake of 1906.

THE STORY OF
AN EYEWITNESS

THE EARTHQUAKE SHOOK DOWN IN SAN FRANCISCO hundreds of thousands of dollars worth of walls and chimneys. But the conflagration that followed burned up hundreds of millions of dollars worth of property. There is no estimating within hundreds of millions the actual damage wrought.

Not in history has a modern imperial city been so completely destroyed. San Francisco is gone. Nothing remains of it but memories and a fringe of dwelling houses on its outskirts. Its industrial section is wiped out. Its business section is wiped out. Its social and residential section is wiped out. The factories and warehouses, the great stores and newspaper buildings, the hotels and the palaces of the nabobs, are all gone. Remains only the fringe of dwelling houses on the outskirts of what was once San Francisco.

Within an hour after the earthquake shock, the smoke of San Francisco's burning was a lurid tower visible a hundred miles away. And for three days and nights this lurid tower swayed in the sky, reddening the sun, darkening the day, and filling the land with smoke.

On Wednesday morning at quarter past five came the earthquake. A minute later the flames were leaping upward. In a dozen different quarters south of Market Street, in the working-class ghetto and in the factories, fires started. There was no opposing the flames. There was no organization, no communication. All the cunning adjustments of a twentieth century city had been smashed by the earthquake. The streets were humped into ridges and depressions, and piled with the debris of fallen walls. The steel rails were twisted into perpendicular and horizontal angles. The telephone and telegraph systems were disrupted. And the great water mains had burst. All the shrewd contrivances and safeguards of man had been thrown out of gear by thirty seconds' twitching of the earth-crust.

By Wednesday afternoon, inside of twelve hours, half the heart of the city was gone. At that time I watched the vast conflagration from out on the bay. It was dead calm. Not a flicker of wind stirred.

Yet from every side wind was pouring in upon the city. East, west, north, and south, strong winds were blowing upon the doomed city. The heated air rising made an enormous suck. Thus did the fire of itself build its own colossal chimney through the atmosphere. Day and night this dead calm continued, and yet, near to the flames, the wind was often half a gale, so mighty was the suck.

Wednesday night saw the destruction of the very heart of the city. Dynamite was lavishly used, and many of San Francisco's proudest structures were crumbled by man himself into ruins, but there was no withstanding the onrush of the flames. Time and again successful stands were made by the firefighters, and every time the flames flanked around on either side, or came up from the rear, and turned to defeat the hard won victory.

An enumeration of the buildings destroyed would be a directory of San Francisco. An enumeration of the buildings undestroyed would be a line and several addresses. An enumeration of the deeds of heroism would stock a library and bankrupt the Carnegie medal fund. An enumeration of the dead—will never be made. All vestiges of them were destroyed by the flames. The number of the victims of the earthquake will never be known. South of Market Street, where the loss of life was particularly heavy, was the first to catch fire.

Remarkable as it may seem, Wednesday night, while the whole city crashed and roared into ruin, was a quiet night. There were no crowds. There was no shouting and yelling. There was no hysteria, no disorder. I passed Wednesday night in the path of the advancing flames, and in all those terrible hours I saw not one woman who wept, not one man who was excited, not one person who was in the slightest degree panic-stricken.

Before the flames, throughout the night, fled tens of thousands of homeless ones. Some were wrapped in blankets. Others carried bundles of bedding and dear household treasures. Sometimes a whole family was harnessed to a carriage or delivery wagon that was weighted down with their possessions. Baby-buggies, toy wagons, and go-carts were used as trucks, while every other person was dragging a trunk. Yet everybody was gracious. The most perfect courtesy obtained. Never, in all San Francisco's history, were her people so kind and courteous as on this night of terror.

All night these tens of thousands fled before the flames. Many of them, the poor people from the labor ghetto, had fled all day as well. They had left their homes burdened with possessions. Now and again they lightened up, flinging out upon the street clothing and treasures they had dragged for miles.

They held on longest to their trunks, and over these trunks many a strong man broke his heart that night. The hills of San Francisco are steep, and up these hills, mile after mile, were the trunks dragged. Everywhere were trunks, with across them lying their exhausted owners, men and women. Before the march of the flames were flung picket-lines of soldiers. And a block at a time, as the flames advanced, these pickets retreated. One of their tasks was to keep the trunk-pullers moving. The exhausted creatures, stirred on by the menace of bayonets, would arise and struggle up the steep pavements, pausing from weakness every five or ten feet.

Often, after surmounting a heart-breaking hill, they would find another wall of flame advancing upon them at right angles and be compelled to change anew the line of their retreat. In the end, completely played out, after toiling for a dozen hours like giants, thousands of them were compelled to abandon their trunks. Here the shop-keepers and soft members of the middle class were at a disadvantage. But the workingmen dug holes in vacant lots and backyards and buried their trunks.

At nine o'clock Wednesday evening, I walked down through the very heart of the city. I walked through miles and miles of magnificent buildings and towering skyscrapers. Here was no fire. All was in perfect order. The police patrolled the streets. Every building had its watchman at the door. And yet it was doomed, all of it. There was no water. The dynamite was giving out. And at right angles two different conflagrations were sweeping down upon it.

At one o'clock in the morning I walked down through the same section. Everything still stood intact. There was no fire. And yet there was a change. A rain of ashes was falling. The watchmen at the doors were gone. The police had been withdrawn. There were no firemen, no fire-engines, no men fighting with dynamite. The district had been absolutely abandoned.

I stood at the corner of Kearney and Market, in the very innermost heart of San Francisco. Kearney Street was deserted. Half a dozen blocks away it was burning on both sides. The street was a wall of flame. And against this wall of flame, silhouetted sharply, were two United States cavalrymen sitting their horses, calmly watching. That was all. Not another person was in sight. In the intact heart of the city two troopers sat their horses and watched.

Surrender was complete. There was no water. The sewers had long since been pumped dry. There was no dynamite. Another fire had broken out farther up-town, and now from three sides conflagrations were sweeping down. The fourth side had been burned earlier in the day. In that direction stood the tottering walls or the *Exam-*

iner Building, the burned out *Call* Building, the smouldering ruins of the Grand Hotel, and the gutted, devastated, dynamited Palace Hotel.

The following will illustrate the sweep of the flames and the inability of men to calculate their spread. At eight o'clock Wednesday evening I passed through Union Square. It was packed with refugees. Thousands of them had gone to bed on the grass. Government tents had been set up, supper was being cooked, and the refugees were lining up for free meals.

At half-past one in the morning three sides of Union Square were in flames. The fourth side, where stood the great St. Francis Hotel, was still holding out. An hour later, ignited from top and sides, the St. Francis was flaming heavenward. Union Square, heaped high with mountains of trunks, was deserted. Troops, refugees, and all had retreated.

It was at Union Square that I saw a man offering a thousand dollars for a team of horses. He was in charge of a truck piled high with trunks from some hotel. It had been hauled here into what was considered safety and the horses had been taken out. The flames were on three sides of the Square, and there were no horses.

Also, at this time, standing beside the truck, I urged a man to seek safety in flight. He was all but hemmed in by several conflagrations. He was an old man and he was on crutches. Said he, "To-day is my birthday. Last night I was worth thirty thousand dollars. I bought five bottles of wine, some delicate fish, and other things for my birthday dinner. I have had no dinner, and all I own are these crutches."

I convinced him of his danger and started him limping on his way. An hour later, from a distance, I saw the truckload of trunks burning merrily in the middle of the street.

On Thursday morning, at quarter past five, just twenty-four hours after the earthquake, I sat on the steps of a small residence on Nob Hill. With me sat Japanese, Italians, Chinese, and Negroes—a bit of the cosmopolitan flotsam of the wreck of the city. All about were the palaces of the nabob pioneers of forty-nine. To the east and south, at right angles, were advancing two mighty walls of flames.

I went inside with the owner of the house on the steps of which I sat. He was cool and cheerful and hospitable. "Yesterday morning," he said, "I was worth six hundred thousand dollars. This morning this house is all I have left. It will go in fifteen minutes." He pointed to a large cabinet. "That is my wife's collection of China. This rug upon which we stand is a present. It cost fifteen hundred dollars. Try that piano. Listen to its tone. There are few like it. There are no horses. The flames will be here in fifteen minutes."

Outside, the old Mark Hopkins residence, a palace, was just catching fire. The troops were falling back and driving the refugees before them. From every side came the roaring of flames, the crashing of walls, and the detonations of dynamite.

I passed out of the house. Day was trying to dawn through the smoke-pall. A sickly light was creeping over the face of things. Once only the sun broke through the smoke-pall, blood-red and showing quarter its usual size. The smoke-pall itself, viewed from beneath, was a rose-color that pulsed and fluttered with lavender shades. Then it turned to mauve and yellow and dun. There was no sun. And so dawned the second day on stricken San Francisco.

An hour later I was creeping past the shattered dome of the City Hall. Than it, there was no better exhibit of the destructive force of the earthquake. Most of the stone had been shaken from the great dome, leaving standing the naked frame-work of steel. Market Street was piled high with the wreckage, and across the wreckage lay the overthrown pillars of the City Hall shattered into short crosswise sections.

This section of the city, with the exception of the Mint and the Post Office, was already a waste of smoking ruins. Here and there through the smoke, creeping warily under the shadows of tottering walls, emerged occasional men and women. It was like the meeting of the handful of survivors after the day of the end of the world.

On Mission Street lay a dozen steers, in a neat row stretching across the street, just as they had been struck down by the flying ruins of the earthquake. The fire had passed through afterward and roasted them. The human dead had been carried away before the fire came. At another place on Mission Street I saw a milk wagon. A steel telegraph pole had smashed down sheer through the driver's seat and crushed the front wheels. The milk cans lay scattered around.

All day Thursday and all Thursday night, all day Friday and Friday night, the flames still raged. Friday night saw the flames finally conquered, though not until Russian Hill and Telegraph Hill had been swept and three-quarters of a mile of wharves and docks had been licked up.

The great stand of the firefighters was made Thursday night on Van Ness Avenue. Had they failed here, the comparatively few remaining houses of the city would have been swept. Here were the magnificent residences of the second generation of San Francisco nabobs, and these, in a solid zone, were dynamited down across the path of the fire. Here and there, the flames leaped the zone, but these isolated fires were beaten out, principally by the use of wet blankets and rugs.

San Francisco, at the present time, is like the crater of a volcano, around which are camped tens of thousands of refugees. At the Presidio alone are at least twenty thousand. All the surrounding cities and towns are jammed with the homeless ones, where they are being cared for by the relief committees. The refugees were carried free by the railroads to any point they wished to go, and it is estimated that over one hundred thousand people have left the peninsula on which San Francisco stood. The government has the situation in hand, and, thanks to the immediate relief given by the whole United States, there is not the slightest possibility of a famine. The bankers and business men have already set about making preparations to rebuild San Francisco.

Sources

Chapter 1.: "The Golden Poppy," *Revolution and Other Essays*. New York: The Macmillan Company, 1910. First published in the New York monthly magazine *The Delineator*, January 1904.

Chapter 2.: *Martin Eden*. New York: The Macmillan Company, 1909. Reprinted over the years by various publishers, including an edition by Holt, Rinehart & Winston that contains an excellent introduction by Sam S. Baskett.

Chapter 3.: *The Valley of the Moon*. New York: The Macmillan Company, 1913.

Chapter 4.: *Burning Daylight*. New York: The Macmillan Company, 1910.

Chapter 5.: "All Gold Canyon," *Moon Face and Other Stories*. New York: The Macmillan Company, 1906.

Chapters 6 and 7.: "A Raid on the Oyster Pirates" and "Demetrios Contos," *Tales of the Fish Patrol*. New York: The Macmillan Company, 1905.

Chapter 8.: "Small-Boat Sailing," *The Human Drift*. New York: The Macmillan Company, 1917.

Chapter 9.: "Navigating Four Horses North of the Bay," *Sunset Magazine*, September 1911.

Chapter 10.: Review of *The Octopus*, *Impressions*, June 1901.

Chapter 11.: "The Story of an Eyewitness," *Collier's Weekly*, May 5, 1906.

Bibliography

NOVELS, AUTOBIOGRAPHICAL WRITING, AND PLAYS

The following chronological list includes works set either wholly or in part in California.

The Cruise of the Dazzler. New York: The Century Co., 1902.

The Call of the Wild. New York: The Macmillan Co., 1903.

The Sea Wolf. New York: The Macmillan Co., 1904.

The Game. New York: The Macmillan Co., 1905.

White Fang. New York: The Macmillan Co., 1906.

The Iron Heel. New York: The Macmillan Co., 1908.

The Abysmal Brute. New York: The Century Co., 1913.

John Barleycorn. (Autobiographical narrative.) New York: The Century Co., 1913.

The Scarlet Plague. New York: The Macmillan Co., 1916.

The Star Rover. New York: The Macmillan Co., 1916.

The Acorn Planter: A California Forest Play. New York: The Macmillan Co., 1916.

The Little Lady of the Big House. New York: The Macmillan Co., 1916.

Michael Brother of Jerry. New York: The Macmillan Co., 1917.

The Assassination Bureau, Ltd. (Completed by Robert L. Fish from notes by Jack London.) New York: McGraw-Hill Book Co., 1963.

SHORT STORY COLLECTIONS AND MISCELLANY

Tales of the Fish Patrol. New York: The Macmillan Co., 1905.

Moon Face and Other Stories. New York: The Macmillan Co., 1907.

Love of Life and Other Stories. New York: The Macmillan Co., 1907.

Revolution and Other Essays. New York: The Macmillan Co., 1910.

When God Laughs and Other Stories. New York: The Macmillan Co., 1911.

The Night Born. New York: The Century Co., 1913.

The Strength of the Strong. New York: The Macmillan Co., 1914.

The Turtles of Tasman. New York: The Macmillan Co., 1916.

The Human Drift. New York: The Macmillan Co., 1917.

The Red One. New York: The Macmillan Co., 1918.

Dutch Courage and Other Stories. New York: The Macmillan Co., 1922.

Jack London Reports. Edited by King Hendricks and Irving Shepard. New York: Doubleday, 1970.